Hearing God's voice in Dreams

Nicholas V. Mbanjwa

© Copyright First edition 2020 – Nicholas V. Mbanjwa

ISBN 9798585283888

Publisher: The Meaning and the Purpose of Life

All rights reserved. No portion of this book may be reproduced, stored in a retrieval system or transmitted in any form or by any means electronic, mechanical, photocopy, recording, or other except for brief quotations in printed reviews, without the prior permission of the author or publisher.

Scripture quotations marked KJV are taken from the King James Version of the Holy Bible, also known as the Authorized Version, 1769.

Scripture quotations marked ASV are taken from the American Standard Version of the Bible, 1901.

Scripture quotations marked CEV are taken from the Contemporary English Version of the Bible © 1995 by American Bible Society.

Scripture quotations marked Darby are taken from the Darby Bible by John Nelson Darby, 1867, 1872, 1884, 1890.

Scripture quotations marked DRB are taken from the Douay Rheims Bible, 1582, 1609, 1752.

Scripture quotations marked ESV are taken from the English Standard Version of the Bible, © Crossway Bibles, and a Publishing ministry of Good News Publishers. All rights reserved.

Scripture quotations marked GW are taken from the God's Word Bible, Copyright © 1995 by GOD'S WORD to the Nations Bible Society. All rights reserved.

Scripture quotations marked Webster are taken from the Webster Common Version, 1833.

Scripture quotations marked Weymouth are taken from the Weymouth New Testament, 1912.

Printed in Johannesburg South Africa

Cover design by Crazy T Designs: 074 033 8567

DEDICATION

To my Wife, the first persistent believer of this work who encouraged me to write a book on dreams since a week hardly passes without receiving a dream to interpret and the avid dreamer I ever met, and to my daughter who lent me the time.

ACKNOWLEDGMENTS

A special thank you goes out to Mr. David Zaze for his extensive knowledge used in the section that concerns the short biography of South Africa's Apostle of faith, Reverend Nicholas Bhengu.

Forever grateful for the first dream interpretation consultation that began nine years ago and that would grow with the years from my former pastor James Chirinda and the House of Prayer at large.

A warm heartfelt gratitude goes to my gorgeous and wise wife for the advices, dreams examples, persistent follow up of the work, planning, vision, market segmentation and analysis which was my challenge, for the outlook design of the book and colors. You are my glory sweetheart, and I will always love you.

Thanks to Bheki Cele our first believer and the first buyer of this book while in the editing process and for assisting us with the necessary resources to put this material to people's hands.

And a thousand praises and gratefulness to my Lord Jesus Christ who has endowed me with the wisdom and grace to interpret and understand dreams. I love my servant King.

Table of Contents

PREFACE ix

Introduction 1

LIFE IS SPIRITUAL 1

PART I: ALL ABOUT DREAMS 4

Chapter 1 5

    13 DREAMS AND THEIR INTERPRETATIONS 5

Chapter 2 13

    WHY DREAMS 13

Chapter 3 17

    WHAT ARE DREAMS MOST ABOUT 17

Chapter 4 20

    WHY ARE DREAMS HIDDEN 20

Chapter 5 22

    THE DIFFERENT TYPES OF DREAMS 22

Chapter 6 25

    DIFFERENCE BETWEEN DREAMS AND VISIONS 25

Chapter 7 33

    ANGELS AND DREAMS 33

Chapter 8 49

    HOW DREAMS HAVE SHAPED THE WORLD 49

Chapter 9 57

DREAMS IN INVENTIONS 57

Chapter 10 66

HOW TO STOP BAD DREAM PREDICTIONS 66

Chapter 11 72

HOW TO HAVE MORE DREAMS AND REMEMBER THEM 72

Chapter 12 78

HOW TO INTERPRET DREAMS Pt 1 78

Chapter 13 97

HOW TO INTERPRET DREAMS Pt2 97

PART II: DREAM BIBLE 107

Symbols of Life and Death in Dreams 108

    Numbers 113

    Colors 126

    Precious Stones and Colors 130

    Clothes 134

        Shoes 141

The Ministry Gifts in Colors 143

Actions in Dreams 145

People in Dreams 154

Animals in Dreams 168

Insects	175
Body Parts in Dreams	179
Places/Buildings in Dreams	185
House	191
Household Essentials	194
Personal Devices/Items	197
Roads in Dreams	200
Nature in Dreams	204
Vegetables	211
Shapes	216
Cardinal Points	218
Water	220
Seasons	222
Transportation	224
On land	224
On Water	225
On Air	226
Weapons	227
TO THE PROPHETS OF DREAMS	229
Bonus Chapter	237

Page intentionally left blank

PREFACE

In 2011 I was homeless and broken. Some members of the community burned my home down. They did this by recruiting a massive number of people to join them in this sadistic act. The accusations were that my late mother was a witch. This was not new such acts are prominent in Africa. I was not present, I was in a Christian camp with my pastor but was later told the whole story.

They searched for a car tire as my late mother drenched in petrol. They wanted to burn her alive. My uncle showed up and pulled her out of the crazed crowd to his taxi as I was later told. That is how she survived. I survived that awful Saturday. My pastor forced me and a few others to join him at a Christian camp the day before. Though reluctant I finally succumbed.

My niece and nephew who were present say it was as if a cloud of blindness had veiled the members of the community. They only awakened to the realization of my uncle speeding off with my mother in the taxi. One of my friends would later remark to me. "All my years in Swaneville of Mayibuye I had never seen the fire brigade but that was for the first time. I wondered what had happened only to find they were coming to you, my friend." A two full-year chase over my mother's and my own life had started.

After all the selfless sacrifices to serve God. Serving people in ministry both the young and old as a youth pastor. I had served in two ministries and of all the daily prayers I had laid out for my family, I asked myself, 'How did this happen? Why did God allow this to happen to me?' Broken, naked, destitute, and confused there I was. This was the beginning of a wearisome mileage of a two-year-long-suffering on my family. Before you were in the position you got yourself into today. If you find yourself in a spiritual drought, social crisis, financial turmoil, marital problems, material lack, or emotional stress there might be yesterday's dream you either heeded or rejected. You may have rejected it because you did not understand. Dreams are God's blessing to everyone. The believing and the unbelieving. I got saved in 2009 on the 29th of March. A few months later I had a troubling dream that I felt was meaningful but could not get around it. I told my Pastor after the interpretation I was still unsatisfied.

I dreamt of walking alongside my Pastor, this was a very long tedious journey. The place where we had this long journey seemed like in Kagiso extension 6. I wasn't wearing shoes in the dream. I noticed the soles of my feet red hot (which my pastor interpreted to mean my walk in Christ's blood). When it meant a journey of suffering. My Pastor was wearing his suit and formal shoes as usual. In the dream, I had the knowledge that he recently had a boy child. At that time my Pastor only had two girls.

We ended up walking on a dusty street. Our road ended up going down steep until we reached the dead-end zone, in front of us was a huge ancient gate. My Pastor and I remained standing in front of the gate, we waited for the gate to open for us. We did not speak a word to each other. It was like there was tension between us. I felt I was weary and tired but my Pastor seemed fine. And the dream ended. On waking up I carried a very weird atmosphere in my spirit that recurred almost the entire day that day. If I had known what I know now I would have negated the outcomes of the dream. And spared my family the long stressful and painful season of hardships.

To my knowledge, I did not know that the process of the journey as seen in the dream was beginning. I took over my High school's Learners' Christian Movement in 2009 it had only five attendees every day. I ran it from Monday to Friday during lunchtimes. Up until it was full to the overflow so much that God began to use me in peculiar ways I had never expected. Demons screaming out of people were cast out. The sick received healing. Many miracles happened and many students gave their lives to Christ. This was new to most of us as I attracted a lot of misinterpretation. Then began persecution from many especially my principal. Things went sore even at home for quite a time.

The following year exhausted me in ministry. I was the youth leader in my church and would take turns to minister on Sundays as my Pastor would request. This was the Pastor in my dreams, Pastor Daniel. Exasperated and feeling anxious about what I'd think was turning to depression. I sought God. And God told me to go back to the House of Prayer. The first church I had committed to before going to Bethel which was my current church at that time. After Pastor Daniel released me, I left for House of Prayer Ministries.

By 2011 on the 26th of November my home was burnt up by the community in Swaneville. By this time, I was submitting under Pastor James in House of Prayer as a youth leader. My mother left for the Eastern Cape Province. I lived with Pastor James and his family. Rumors went about that the instigators of my burnt house sought after my life. My mother called my former Pastor Daniel to take me in since he lived in Kagiso a different city. This was the place of the journey according to my 2009 dream. It was also extension 6 though in the dream the extension 6 I saw was a different one.

The number 6 also implies the number of men. A place can mean a situation in dreams meaning I was to be into this situation by men, not by God. It was the hand of the devil through people that brought me to the 2011 dilemma. And so I left to live with him, Pastor Daniel. I brought along my nephew who was still in High school. My niece moved in with her mother, my sister to Boksburg, the east side of Johannesburg. Those were the hardest and most testing times in my life. In spiritual, emotional, and financial areas. By this time Pastor Dan's wife was pregnant. I was again helping the Pastor in the ministry as I assumed the church leadership. Things took another turn. The mountain I was climbing seemed to be insurmountable. A breakthrough came in by this time it was 2015 April. My nephew and I found a place.

I brought my mother from the Eastern Cape to come live with us. Pastor Dan's wife was to give birth to a baby boy and right there I remembered the dream. This is where my Pastor's path and mine took different turns. The dream ended with me not seeing it to the end. We were still standing in front of the gate. When a dream ends not seen to the end, having any conclusion. This implies that God is leaving the rest of the predictions of the dream to our experience. This also implies that the participant's will is to decide the outcomes.

` From then on I vowed to approach dreams with a new perspective and pray on them. In this book, I am going to be communicating a language familiar to dreamers and prophets of visions. In case you find it hard. Many will receive a pearl of supernatural wisdom, understanding, and knowledge on how to interpret dreams through this material.

This book should be your lifelong mentor, adviser, and friend as you dream on to destiny. Keep it by your bedside with a journal to record and date down all the dreams you feel are important. When you travel take it along dreams are never home-bound.

Introduction

LIFE IS SPIRITUAL

There is nothing such as, 'it was a mere dream,' over 80% of our dreams are spiritual if not soulish. In the year 2014, my previous pastor James Chirinda and a brother of mine in the Lord, and I took an itinerary. Our journey led us to Limpopo Province of South Africa to a village called Seloane in Phalaborwa. Pastor Peter Mathebula who was Pastor's assistant had opened a branch there. We went there to establish it. We held a seven days revival meeting it was to begin on a Monday until Sunday. Most of the church leadership from Joburg would join us on that given Friday.

That Monday pastor ministered and he asked me to take the following day which was to be a Tuesday. It was a tent packed to capacity as I ministered. The Lord had touched me to minister on the message of the blood and the covenant. I dwelt on Rahab and the two spies that is Joshua chapter 2. I drew the congregant's attention to the faith of Rahab. Her words on the report their land had heard of the God of the Israelites. The red cord she agreed to tie on her window as a covenant between her and the spies she hid in her house.

The red cord symbolized the blood, the covenant between the spies and her. I proceeded to proclaim the efficacy of the blood of the Lamb. The entire household of Rahab got protected and saved through the red cord when God caused the entire walls of Jericho to come down tumbling. I built so much faith around the audience that after I finished ministering I called a healing line. Before I called the healing line I had a Word of Knowledge about a woman who had a tumor on her left breast. I later learned I called for her though I did not remember after that. I was so taken by the atmosphere of the presence of the Holy Spirit that I had no notion of whatsoever.

Hearing God's voice in Dreams

The healing line was so great that it stretched from one end of the tent to the other. I invited Pastor James and the brother we came with to help me minister to the sick. I took the left wing of the healing line. The woman I had called for came to my side. We had a language barrier, during ministering Pastor was the interpreter. I reached the woman when one of the ushering ladies made it known to me that that is the woman I had called for. I asked her about the problem she told me of the breast tumor. It was under her breast as big as a baby's hand.

I stopped the service and drew the whole attention to the woman. I asked both of my lady ushers to touch the tumor under her breast and tell the church about it. One of them jumped from fright upon feeling it. Immediately, I received supernatural boldness that I do not know why I said what I said. In boldness, I said to her over the speakers in English, "I will lay hands on you and this tumor will leave you right NOW!" One of my ushers translated that in Xitsonga. She nodded. I immediately put one hand on her back and the other on her chest. I growled as one usher held the mic for me, "Come out NOW in Jesus' Name!" She stooped over and vomited once and then twice while her other hand reached for her breast. She did not have to say a word as she screamed in Xitsonga (her native language). Straightening back up with tears streaming down her dark chicks. The whole church erupted in a rain of praises. After she stopped praying we asked the ladies to feel the tumor under her breast it was gone.

On that Sunday during the hour of testimonies, she stood up to testify. We learned as the church that on that Tuesday the tumor was worse painful she had to force herself to the meeting. In her own words, she told us it was in 2006 when she had a dream. In the dream, she saw herself waking up to find a man in her bedroom. Wearing a mask carved out of cow fur with pierced holes for eyes. The man in the dream said not a single word but pulled out another fur of a cow. He began scratching it with his nails which action caused her to feel an itch under her left breast. The more she scratched the more it itched. This continued for a while until a tumor developed. Such stories are typical in Africa as many others were also poisoned in dreams. This woman was what we call a member of a Zion sect. This group blinds people into believing that they are worshipping God. When in truth they are deep into ancestry worship. Many feel they can't leave them as they believe these are African aboriginal worships. And that they'd be deserting their true African traditions.

To study what the Bible says about ancestry worship see the eleventh chapter of my book, The Prophecy. The woman came with her Zion worship clothes to burn them that Sunday (Acts. 19: 19) and she gave her life to Jesus with tears of joy. We saw many other miracles during the meetings. We glorified God.

Whether you believe this or not but dreams are almost anything but spiritual. If we don't control our lives in the spirit we are sure to face defeat. Among the many things you will learn in this book, one, in particular, will be how to stop bad dream predictions. In part one of this book, we will cover everything that has to do with dreams. Like where they come from, why they are symbolic, and how to interpret them. And in the second part of this book, we will cover what colors, numbers, clothes, shoes, certain people, actions, places/buildings, items, and seasons mean in dreams.

When you read any book for the first time you get knowledge of the title. But reading it for the second time you get an understanding of the title. You should at least read the whole book more than once. If you can't, then read the chapters 'How to interpret dreams part 1 and 2'. Reading those chapters at least three times you will get the hang of how to interpret dreams better.

PART I: ALL ABOUT DREAMS

Chapter 1

13 DREAMS AND THEIR INTERPRETATIONS

1. Shoe dream

Dream: (Grace) *when I was looking for shoes I saw shoes that were muddy and white*

Interpretation: all right shoes mean an assignment or your walk of faith. This means you are in doubt about your assignment and before you are two things you are considering. One is what you think is your calling and people think is your calling which might bog you down and lead you to sin (mud). The second one is the right calling the Lord has for you which will lead you to true worship and purity (white shoes). This is a warning dream from the Lord. You should be diligent in making the right decision since you are more likely to make a mistake.

2. Breeding nose dream

Dream: (Grace) *I dreamt my nose breeding and my tongue had rolled I was praying for forgiveness.*

Interpretation: all right, the nose means anger or wrath from the Bible Hebrew *aph*. The Lord is revealing this to you so you deal with your growing anger. This anger will affect your influence, spiritual judgment, and perception (your tongue).

3. Unripe mangoes dream

Hearing God's voice in Dreams

Dream: *I dreamed I was plucking unripe mangoes for my family members. And I pluck a big cucumber in a mango tree and I wondered how that can be possible, interpretation pls.*

Interpretation: Hi, a tree means your job or business. Fruits like mango mean success or work of your labor. You plucked up unripe mangoes for your family members. This means any time from now you might find yourself in an awkward position of withdrawing from the little success you currently have. You might be in a position to try to help out your family members from your seed. What you should be doing instead is waiting until your job or business is stable enough to bring lasting success worth sharing (ripe mangoes). Instead, this will discourage you as your business or job will produce results unexpected or less than what you'd bargain for.

4. Flying dream

Dream: (Kingsley) *I dreamt I was going somewhere on the road. Howbeit, I was not walking but flying above the ground. I reached a point where the roads crossed each other like this +. I looked to the left side of the road I noticed a few people in a house slinging stones to the by-passers of the road. So due to fear, nobody was passing. I then flew to that house while flying on air I warned them that threw stones to the road to stop people from passing. And I asked them if don't they know that people are passing on that road. After the warning, I left as I reached their gate it looked as if they used a remote to lock the gate in front of me. I marched three times before the gate and it opened for me, as I flew out they again started throwing stones at me but none of the stones touched me. I then reached the junction and began to tell people to begin to pass on that road. I told them that not a single stone will hit them, and they began to pass and not a single stone touched anyone.*

Interpretation: All right, that's very detailed. Walking in this dream means a journey you are about to embark on, what is about to happen in your life shortly. You were not walking but flying, this means God is calling you to a prophetic office. Crossroads means you will come across a moment where you will have to make a major decision about your future. This will be whether you choose to continue the road for yourself or you help others. But you decided to help people. The challenges faced by you and your people are forces that are intended to cripple them in life (stones). You are thus endued with the ability to oppose these forces through your gift (taking the left road). Entering their gates, the enemies' gates mean that your calling also includes you're invading the space of authority of these forces. And then leading the ones, the people who will be willing to follow the same route you once traveled. Because of your mentorship, they will also conquer and win as you did.

"You are right, a man entered my shop one day, and called me a prophet, and said the Lord has made me a prophet already, he prayed for me and left." These were the dreamer's confirmation words.

5. Pregnancy dream

Dream: (Ayodele) *I had a dream that I was pregnant though in reality I am still a virgin likewise in the dream. So I was asking myself how I got pregnant without sex, to cut it short I gave birth to a baby girl.*

Interpretation: Being pregnant in this instance speaks of being spiritually pregnant (being loaded). Giving birth to a baby girl speaks of a ministry gift that God has recently given you. You are thus responsible to nurture and grow it.

6. Getting married dream

Dream: (Sakwe) *I had a dream of getting married. I was standing next to the guy holding hands and in front of the priest and people. I was wearing a beautiful white dress it had small diamonds on it and it was sparkling. I was very happy it felt real I didn't even want to wake up.*

Interpretation: This is a beautiful dream. Africans would tell you it's a bad dream but according to the Bible, it is a good one. What it means, it reveals a great journey ahead of your life a pure (white gown). But this journey will need your commitment to seeing it through hence the wedding. Diamonds mean the process of pain and hurt you have gone through. Diamonds form out of the intense pressures under the earth. Meaning the things you went through, God will use them to make something great out of your life. God brings such dreams when you at a point of discouragement. Holding hands means you are already in contact with this blessing coming on to your life. But do bear in mind that it will only come to pass with commitment. You will also need to put effort on your side like marriage needs commitment and work.

This was her comment in her own words: *"Ah oh my word and I've been so discouraged. This means a lot."*

7. Fetching cars dream

Dream: (Siya) *I dreamt of my Grandma, she's passed on... so like all my family members were there and my grandma was telling us to fetch these particular cars. It was a lot of them in our small garage and I was asking myself where all these cars are going to fit... my mom and I were the ones fetching them and bringing them home. Then there were a lot of people feasting on something very delicious.*

Interpretation: this dream is about your family and you guys. The things that are affecting you. Cars mean destinies or personal gifts, it can be jobs or businesses in this context. You picked them and parked them in a small garage. Meaning you fall prey to taking all that is at your disposal and limiting it down (putting them into a small garage). This is what brings you to stagnancy (garage, a place where cars park).

You need to pray against imminent death too in your family (the being together part plus eating).

Hearing God's voice in Dreams

8. Boyfriend's place dream

Dream: (Siya) *I dreamt I was at my boyfriend's place, I was visiting then he pulled a drawer with large bras in it they were color red and blue... suddenly my brother was there sitting on the bed. In the room ants were making a small mountain with the sand... my brother then put out his hand on top of the mountain then it became a hole I then called my sister who is a Nyanga (witch doctor) in training to come to look then I woke up...*

Interpretation: All right, I only interpret dreams using Scriptures. To begin with, the dream is not about you but your boyfriend. Secondly, this type of dream is a vision, a vision to his life as you were in his room. A drawer means issues of the heart. There are women issues he hasn't resolved in his life. And as a result, he sometimes finds it hard to fit in your relationship (the bras were large). A brother in this context speaks of the Lord Jesus. You may have prayed for this relationship and now the Lord is revealing something. So he set upon his bed which means in his life there is an aspect of faith in Christ. Now ants here mean demonic forces. These demonic forces are working to destruct his productivity and ideas in life.

They disturb and distract his peace (red) with so much stress and inner conflict (blue). And even affect his relationships. These little problems are beginning to form a huge problem that he might find hard to surmount. Its results may be death in his family and things surrounding his life.

(Siya): His Grandma died last night and I was struggling to believe him...

9. Fluorescent eyes dream

Dream: (Maria) *I had a dream that my eyes turned into gemstones. They were so pretty and resembled labradorite fluorescent color. What does it mean?*

Hearing God's voice in Dreams

Interpretation: Eyes in dreams reveal insight and perception. In this context, they reveal spiritual insight and perception. This means the situation you are in in your life at the moment is there not to destroy. It will but bring out greater spiritual insight, perception, experience, and wisdom. Gemstones form out of intense pressure under the earth's surface. This means your insight and wisdom will be born from transient hardships and trials. And this also means you will come out of that situation glorious.

God is not the author of sufferings but the devil that tricked the fall (see James 1:17, *"Every good and perfect gift comes from above, from the Father of lights."*). Any dream surrounded by lights or bright colors reveals God as the source. The situation (hardship, trial) might not be from God. But the gift of spiritual insight, perception, and wisdom that you will gain out of that situation will be a gift from Him.

10. New baby and thick milk dream

Dream: (Anonymous) *I dreamt of having a new child. The milk I was giving to the child was too thick for the child.*

Interpretation: A new child means a new ministry, relationship, job, or project. Milk is a product of nutrients generated by the food a mother eats. In this case, the new project of this person is bound to die as long as she focuses on investing in it without her aligning priorities. The most important priority here is her than the child (new venture). If a mother needs rich milk for her baby she has to eat rich and healthy food. So if she wants her new project to survive she needs to invest in herself first. Invest in herself like studying books, researching more, and preparing herself for the project at hand). The healthier she gets the great the success of her new project will stand.

Side note: Based on the feedback of the dreamer this spoke of a new job because she had had an interview the last Friday of the dream.

11. Bitten by a snake dream

Hearing God's voice in Dreams

Dream: (Ishmael) *I dreamt of a snake biting me on my right wrist three times and its color was gray. Its venom didn't affect me. I shut it into a lunchbox that had a gray lid because I wanted to present it to the hospital for an antidote. I could not make up my mind about a hospital from the 3 in my head and I ended up not going to any of them.*

Interpretation: Your right wrist represents your surrender and God-given authority (the right-hand side). Being bitten by a gray snake (this means you attacked by a satanic lie that seeks to alter what you know about God and His ways, your identity in Christ). A snake means a lie (you saw it big but after the effect, you realized it's a small snake). This lie seemed big upon approaching but after the consequences, you will realize it's nothing but a small issue. The venom didn't affect you (consequences). This snake being gray was a satanic attack, lie of the devil to attack your assignment and matters of identity in Christ (gray= your spiritual growth). Instead, you shut it into a lunchbox with the same color. This means you still carry the wound and this experience with you to this moment.

Yet, you do realize that you need a healing ministry to help you heal from that experience (hospitals). You had an idea of the ones that would help you (ministries or ministers). But the problem is that you still haven't made up your mind on which one to go to.

12. Parked car dream

Dream: (Sonti) *I dreamt of visiting a certain church in Cosmo City (Johannesburg). The Pastor of that church was closing the gate as I was about to go in. So he looked at me then he opened the gate for me to go in. Then I went inside and parked the car and went inside the church. But inside I couldn't find the chair until another Pastor called me to come to sit next to him.*

Do you think this dream has spiritual significance?

Interpretation: The dream does have spiritual significance. It shows there is a certain Pastor you believe in, with whom you will have a relationship soon. But things will take a different turn because he will not have a place for you in his ministry. There will be a pastor after that that will make you his assistant at the expense of your ministry (as you parked your car, ministry).

13. carrying the cross dream

Dream: (Prince) *I was praying a few weeks ago about ministry clarity. A certain man of God I hadn't seen in a long time happened to visit me because he had had a dream about me. In his dream, he said, he saw me carrying a very big cross on my shoulders walking with it. As I was carrying this cross, he saw that people were laughing at me as though I was a joke. And he said I immediately stopped and said, "I established a ministry." Saying this not to them but rather generally saying it. He then said after I uttered those words everyone stopped laughing and kept quiet as though they couldn't say anything.*

Interpretation: Generally, a taking of the cross upon one's self means to follow Christ. It means one's sacrifice, and love for Him. Your shoulders mean responsibility, this being your responsibility. He saw you carrying the cross walking, this means what's happening right now in your life (walking). People were laughing at you as though you were a joke. This means whatever you are right now eluding many and it hasn't appeared will you will be. But immediately when you begin to accept the call and own it God will begin to release you to a certain level. A level of authority that you will be so feared and honored. Even the ones who never appreciated you before but were only observing your life will honor you. This ministry is more than a prophetic office but has an aura of leadership with it. In the future, it will lean more toward the apostolic. Judging by the authority you exhibit through your presence. The dream also reveals that you won't ever make sense of your life until you do what the Lord wants you to do.

Chapter 2

WHY DREAMS

In the entire Scriptures concerning God speaking to us nowhere does He ever become emphatic to say that He speaks to us in dreams except in only two verses because throughout the New Testament Scriptures we are only told God leads us through our spirits (Rom. 8:14-16, 9:1, 1 Joh. 2:27, 5:10). He also speaks to us through our intuition or you can call it the inward witness. But of the two verses concerning God speaking to us in dreams the one below is more direct:

> *God speaks in one way, even in two ways without people noticing it: In a dream, a prophetic vision at night, when people fall into a deep sleep, when they sleep on their beds, he opens people's ears and terrifies them with warnings. He warns them to turn away from doing wrong and to stop being arrogant. He keeps their souls from the pit and their lives from crossing the River of Death.* (Job 33:14-18 GW)

"He said, "Listen to my words: When there are prophets of the LORD among you, I make myself known to them in visions or speak to them in dreams." (Num. 12:6 GW).

Ways God leads us according to the order of their priority

- The Word
- Still small voice
- Intuition/inward witness
- Visions
- Dreams

The Purpose of Dreams

Important: Do not let dreams lead you, they should only guide you. The Bible says God leads us in the New Testament through our spirits (Rom. 8:14-16), below are reasons why He speaks to us through dreams:

1. The Bible says God speaks to us through our dreams. Dreams are like billboards that show us where we are, where we going, and how far from God's will or destiny are we. God does exhort us through dreams.

2. They also serve as a way of warning concerning the wrong soulish motives, *"He warns them to turn away from doing wrong and to stop being arrogant. He keeps their souls from the pit and their lives from crossing the River of Death."* Job 33:17-18 GW.

3. God does also protect us through dreams, Mat. 2:12 GW, *"God warned them in a dream not to go back to Herod. So they left for their country by another road."* Mat 2:13 GW, *"After they had left, an angel of the Lord appeared to Joseph in a dream. The angel said to him, "Get up, take the child and his mother, and flee to Egypt. Stay there until I tell you, because Herod intends to search for the child and kill him."*

We are always in between roads about the job to take, who to marry, where to live, whether to relocate or not, the right business partner, where to render our service. When we pray and ask God concerning any of the above choices we are to expect to receive the answer in our spirits and have our dreams confirm it. God wills to communicate with each one of us directly than through a prophet or a pastor.

By this, I do not imply dreams in a Prophets office but personal dreams. When we get to chapter 6 *The Difference between Dreams and Visions*, we will distinguish the difference.

God speaking in dreams in the Bible

Abraham

Hearing God's voice in Dreams

In Genesis 15, God, before making a covenant with Abraham; told him to bring a three-year-old heifer, a three-year-old female goat, a three-year-old ram, a mourning dove, and a pigeon. After Abram had cut the heifer, the goat, and ram in half the Bible records that a deep sleep fell upon Abram. This is where he saw the 500 years of his descendants in a dream. 450 years in Egypt and the 50 years of possessing the land. I do not dispute the fact that God told him about 400 years of slavery in Egypt.

Abimelech

When he had taken Abraham's wife God warned him in a dream, Gen 20:3-5 GW, *"God came to Abimelech in a dream one night and said to him, "You're going to die because of the woman that you've taken! She's a married woman!" Abimelech hadn't come near her, so he asked, "Lord, will you destroy a nation even if it's innocent? Didn't he tell me himself, 'She's my sister,' and didn't she even say, 'He's my brother'? I did this in all innocence and with a clear conscience."*

Jacob

When Jacob usurped the blessing his father intended to release upon Esau he (Jacob) then ran from his homeland when his brother Esau in anger sought to kill him. The sun went down on his travel when he was at Luz. He stayed to sleep with his head rested upon a stone. He fell into a dream where he saw a portal to heaven. A long ladder reaching to heaven, angels ascending and descending. On top of the ladder was the Lord. The Lord made a promise to him and when he woke up, he made a vow to the Lord. The course of his destiny was forever altered in this experience.

Pharaoh

Pharaoh had two dreams that foresaw the seven years of famine that came upon the land of Egypt. History shelves are packed with books of kings that foresaw national crisis and inventors that had inventions born through dreams as we shall explore.

Gideon

Gideon and the Israelites when faced by the plundering and incessant incursions of the Midianites God provided him with a dream to strengthen his courage concerning they're short to be experienced victory over the enemies of Israel.

Solomon

It was in a dream where God asked him of anything He could give him. Solomon woke up the next morning the wisest king who ever lived and the richest king who ever braced the sands of history.

We have many other examples even in the New Testament we won't get into right now.

Chapter 3

WHAT ARE DREAMS MOST ABOUT

One of the important foundations I understood on how to understand and interpret dreams was from the writings of Van Niekerk. This mainly brings down a dream to the subject's dominant thoughts before the occurrence of the dream. This means whatever your dream today is an answer to what you have been worried about, contemplating, or meditating on. Let's view a few Scriptures as proof of that.

Eph. 3:20 GW, *"Glory belongs to God, whose power is at work in us. By this power he can do infinitely more than we can ask or imagine."* The simplest form to the comprehension of faith is understanding that any man in Christ has within him or herself the resurrection power. This power has everything to do with our lives living in supernatural manifestations and providence. Christianity is anything but faith in the supernatural. Jesus died and on the third day, God raised Him from the dead. That is the greatest miracle in the eternity of ages.

Apostle Paul witnesses the tremendous exploits that power can achieve. He had died and was raised back to life by that power (see 2 Cor. 12:1-4). In the above verse, he expresses that the power at work within us can do infinitely more than we can ask or imagine. Whether we pray or imagine ourselves through any situation that power is able to perform in imagination as it does in prayer. Meaning whatever as children of God we face God gives us answers via our dreams. This does not apply of course to those who do not have the Spirit of Life abiding in them. They may dream themselves more into problems and confusion.

Joseph was engaged to Mary when he discovered her pregnant having known her as a virgin. Being a just man he decided to put her away privily without drawing shame to her. Matt. 1:20 GW, *"Joseph had this in mind when an angel of the Lord appeared to him in a dream. The angel said to him, "Joseph, descendant of David, don't be afraid to take Mary as your wife. She is pregnant by the Holy Spirit."* Every word or description in the Bible is by deliberate design. The details are not just to paint vivid pictures in our minds but each detail has a hidden meaning. If a verse lets us know of a certain garment's color the Bible character was wearing you should know there is a revelation and a deeper meaning behind that detail. The above verse states that Joseph had these things in mind concerning Mary. He thought about these things and then having them in his mind God sent an angel to tell him to take Mary for she was pregnant by the Holy Spirit.

    King Nebuchadnezzar having achieved the greatest achievements as witnessed in the history of that known world. He built an empire, established the most powerful nation, and amassed so much wealth and fame that he became perplexed over the future of his kingdom. Dan. 2:29 GW, *'Your Majesty, while you were lying in bed, thoughts about what would happen in the future came to you. The one who reveals secrets told you what is going to happen."* As the king had thoughts concerning the future God answered him in a dream. This is the dream about the famous gigantic statue that foretold the succession of three other kings who would succeed king Nebuchadnezzar. The words of Daniel add more weight to this context, *"But as for me, this secret is not revealed to me for any wisdom that I have more than any living, but for their sakes that shall make known the interpretation to the king, and that thou mightiest know the **thoughts of thy heart**."* Dan. 2:30 KJV.

    Paul when he had left Timothy in Macedonia where he met a violent opposition that he traveled to Corinth. In reaching Corinth he was fearful but he did not let fear get on his way to preaching the Gospel. 1 Cor. 2:3 GW, *"When I came to you, I was weak. I was afraid and very nervous."* By the look of things, this fear did not leave Paul for a long time even after he began to see little promises of his labor. Acts 18:9 GW, *"One night the Lord said to Paul in a vision, "Don't be afraid to speak out! Don't be silent!"* The Lord delivered him through a word in a dream from the little voices in his head.

Dreams are sometimes an answer from God concerning something we have asked him, 1Sa. 28:6 GW, *"He prayed to the LORD, but the LORD didn't answer him through dreams, the Urim, or prophets."* In the Old Testament among the three mediums, God communicated to His people dreams were the first option. We know this because of the first law of mention. In the above verse, dreams are mentioned before the Urim or the prophet

Chapter 4

WHY ARE DREAMS HIDDEN

Take for instance the parables, Jesus spoke more in parables than in plain language. His sole reason for why He spoke in parables answers us why He speaks through dreams with hidden meanings. The Lord uses dreams because of these five reasons:

1. He spoke mysteries of the Kingdom to an audience that was not yet ready for them. As a result, the Lord hid the meaning behind the parable. And when later they'd be ready then they would understand the meaning of the parable.
2. God rewards the diligent, there is a reward for anyone who searches the hidden secrets of the Kingdom, Pro. 25:2 GW, *"It is the glory of God to hide things but the glory of kings to investigate them."*
3. To lessen our accountability. Should a thing be revealed to you, you are held accountable. Lk. 12:48 GW, *"...A lot will be expected from everyone who has been given a lot. More will be demanded from everyone who has been entrusted with a lot."* If God reveals a dream to you and you understand it, you will be held accountable in case you did not do what you were told. In the Kingdom God will discipline individuals that will not have produced fruits (see Matt. 18:34), the more accountable the severe the discipline, I deal more on this topic in my book The Prophecy.
4. To hide mysteries from those who are not of the Kingdom.
5. Spiritual language is hard to be understood and explained thus God uses elements and methods we are acquainted with for us to grasp His message.

To you, it is given to understand Mysteries

The disciples asked him, "Why do you use stories as illustrations when you speak to people?" Jesus answered, "Knowledge about the mysteries of the kingdom of heaven has been given to you. But it has not been given to the crowd. Those who understand these mysteries will be given more knowledge, and they will excel in understanding them. However, some people don't understand these mysteries. Even what they understand will be taken away from them. (Matt. 13:10-12 GW).

In God's Kingdom, the Lord expects us to be zealous and that that zeal acquires knowledge. Each of us is called to bear fruits, Joh. 15:5 GW, *"I am the vine. You are the branches. Those who live in me while I live in them will produce a lot of fruit. But you can't produce anything without me."* We are enabled with every possible gifting and anointing to produce fruits. We were expected to produce lasting fruits to God before the fall. In Genesis chapter 1 God blessed the male and the female to be fruitful and to multiply. It depends on an individual to understand mysteries because Jesus says to understand mysteries is given to us.

I want to call your attention to understanding this, mysteries were until Christ came. The word mysteries in the New Testament means in the Greek that which has been hidden but now has been revealed. If any believer fails to comprehend any mystery in the Bible that is a failure due to him or her not studying the Scriptures diligently. God has done everything He could about it. Col. 1:26 & 27 GW, *"In the past God hid this mystery, but now he has revealed it to his people. ... the glorious riches of this mystery-which is Christ living in you, giving you the hope of glory."* Every mystery is solved in the revelation of Christ. In my deep and diligent study of Christ, I found myself able to interpret dreams more easily.

Chapter 5

THE DIFFERENT TYPES OF DREAMS

Godly Dreams (God)

How do you know a dream is from God? Let's give an example. Let's say you dream fighting and toward the end of the dream, you win or overpower your opponent. The context of such a dream is godly in that it aligns with the Scriptures, you overcome. Godly type of dreams have these characteristics following them:

- They are filled with lights or colors
- They are destiny focused
- Enhance or reveal you to the knowledge of the Word of God
- Build hope
- Stir up faith
- Arouse reverence toward God
- Call you to prayer
- Bring you to a realization of worship

Intercessory Dreams: This is any dream where you dream of carrying someone you know or helping a feeble person walk, dreaming of a clinic, hospital, ministry, any building, or a system that services people or a community. Or dreaming not being alone but with someone else in the dream but this also depends on the context of the dream.

Prophetic Dreams: This is any dream where you dream of watching a TV, listening to a radio, receiving a text on your mobile phone, computer screen, beating a drum, playing trumpet, carrying a horn, having an anointing oil, viewing from a mountain top, pointing your index finger. We will deal more with this one in the following chapter.

Warning Dreams: This is any dream where you dream of any animal, the context has to be negative. Say maybe you dream of playing with a snake and then it bites you. This is a warning dream. God might be warning you of a certain individual's deception, lie, or impending danger. Again, I have to emphasize, context is important to determine whether a dream is a warning dream. It does not always have to have animals in it. Sometimes warning dreams have authority personnel in them, a traffic officer, soldier, a judge, a police officer, or a government official these all mean that there is a spiritual law that you have violated and God wants you to fix it. Unless they are fighting for you or helping you then in that context heavenly beings are defending you. If a judge decrees a verdict in your favor this means heaven has decreed an order for you against a certain situation.

All the above godly dreams have their source as God.

Demonic Dreams (Satan)

Demonic dreams are distinguishable by their occurring at night, dark colors, grey color, stuck in the mud, dirty water, and swamp, caged or in a cell and when you wake up from a demonic dream you will realize it was a demonic dream based on feeling fearful, chaotic, confused or troubled in your spirit. These dreams do occasionally have animals in them as well. And such dreams tend to make you suspicious of someone. Mark the difference between a warning from someone and suspicion of someone. When you wake up feeling fearful, confused, or troubled this is a call for you to pray because it can swing your moods backward for the rest of your day.

Demonic dreams and spiritual warfare dreams have their origin from Satan and his demons.

Spiritual Warfare Dreams

A spiritual warfare dream has to do with you being chased by someone, something, or a certain group of people, fighting, wrestling, arguing, avoiding falling into the water, etc.

Soulish Dreams

You will know you had a soulish dream if it was in line with your lustful imaginations, or a dream that enhanced your reasoning and fleshly lusts or affections. These types of dreams originate from the unconscious mind. Sigmund Freud, a psychoanalyst, often refers to the unconscious as *"a mind that has a will and purpose of its own"*. He further says that the subconscious is a repository (storage) for socially unacceptable ideas, wishes or desires, traumatic memories, and painful emotions put out of mind by the mechanism of psychological repression. These have been more evident in youthful lusts when a male has an experience in Biology termed as wet dreams. Sometimes as soulish dreams that ultimately achieve in youth passions known as crush alike in both males and females.

Chapter 6

DIFFERENCE BETWEEN DREAMS AND VISIONS

We will have to start with visions so you understand the meaning of dreams that are visions. This will help you understand better especially when God is beginning to use you in prophetic visions. Before we deal with visions, we will first arrange two of the revelation gifts. Namely, the Word of Wisdom and the Word of Knowledge. As some of us know, the manifestations of the Spirit total nine gifts of the Spirit divided into three categories, refer to 1 Cor. 12:8-10:

Revelation Gifts

1. Word of Wisdom
2. Word of Knowledge
3. Discerning of spirits

Inspiration Gifts

1. Prophecy
2. Different kinds of Tongues
3. Interpretation of Tongues

Power Gifts

1. Word of Faith (miracles producing faith)
2. Gifts of Healings
3. Working of Miracles

For this study, we will only focus on the revelation gifts. The word of wisdom, the word of knowledge, and the discerning of spirits. We will begin with the Word of Wisdom. The Bible mentions it first. The law of the first mention.

The Word of wisdom: a revelation of God's plans and purposes that concern the future. Normally this vision will include a solution. An example is found in Acts 11:27-30 GW, *"At that time some prophets came from Jerusalem to the city of Antioch. One of them was named Agabus. Through the Spirit, Agabus predicted that a severe famine would affect the entire world. This happened while Claudius was emperor. All the disciples in Antioch decided to contribute whatever they could afford to help the believers living in Judea. The disciples did this and sent their contribution through Barnabas and Saul to the leaders in Jerusalem."*

The Word of knowledge: a revelation concerning any particular place, person, or situation that might have happened in the past or happening presently: 2 Kings 5:21-27 GW. 3

So Gehazi went after Naaman. When Naaman saw Gehazi running after him, he got down from his chariot to speak to him. "Is something wrong?" he asked. Gehazi answered, "No. My master has sent me. He says, 'Just now two young men from the disciples of the prophets in the hills of Ephraim have arrived. Please give them 75 pounds of silver and two sets of clothing.'" Naaman replied, "Please let me give you 150 pounds of silver." Naaman urged him to take the silver. Naaman tied up 150 pounds of silver in two bags with two sets of clothing. He gave them to a couple of his servants to carry in front of Gehazi. When Gehazi came to the Ophel in Samaria, he took these things and put them away in the house. Then he dismissed the men, and they left. He went and stood in front of his master. Elisha asked him, "Where were you, Gehazi?" "I didn't go anywhere," he answered. Then Elisha said to him, "I went with you in spirit when the man turned around in his chariot to speak to you. How could you accept silver, clothes, olive orchards, vineyards, sheep, cattle, or slaves? Naaman's skin disease will cling to you and your descendants permanently!" When he left Elisha, Gehazi had a disease that made his skin as flaky as snow.

Discerning of spirits: seeing and hearing into the realm of the spirit. Through this gift, one can see what is influencing a certain action on someone or what is influencing certain situations. Here is an example of a dream that falls under discerning of spirits: A year ago (2019) one of the ladies at church approached me concerning her prayer for a job. This was after a Sunday church service. She said to me she has been praying to God to get a job for over a year now. She had graduated and was seeking a job for over a year. Her family is not saved and so they continually discouraged her, they even insisted that she do a certain act for luck, whatever it is it is just not biblically based. She boldly said to me looking sternly into my eyes that she never once had an ounce of doubt. I held her hands and prayed with her. I prayed the prayer of faith and she received. I told her to take note of the dreams she'd dream that night.

On the following Monday morning, she sent me a message about a dream she dreamt that night. In her dream, she dreamt of a snake in her bad room. It had black and yellow colors. This was God using a dream to show her that God had done all He could do about the situation. It was only a demonic spirit that stood in the way of her receiving her job. This type of dream is a revelation dream it reveals the cause of her situation which categorizes the dream as discerning of spirits. God gave us all the authority over demonic spirits that now leaves Him out of the equation. I continued telling her that the type of spirit that was standing on her breakthrough was a spirit of ignorance (black) and greed (yellow). I told her to shut her bedroom door behind her and pray like this, *"You spirit of ignorance and greed standing on my way to receiving my job I command you to stay out of my way of finding my job and out of my way of prosperity in Jesus' Name. Go ministering spirits (angels) and bring me back my intended job this week in Jesus' Name."*

Hearing God's voice in Dreams

I told her to only pray that once for if she'd pray that again the second time she'd be walking in unbelief. Not sure about the details of days between her receiving the call that it was the same day or the next day, Tuesday, but all I remember is that she got a call sooner, it did not take two days. By Wednesday she had two job interviews on her table. One was under a contract and the other was a permanent post.

This goes to mean that visions of the night concerning the future and God's purposes fall under the word of wisdom. Visions of the night concerning the past fall under a word of knowledge. Visions of the night concerning demonic activity around your life fall under the discerning of spirits, refer to the title *Animals in Dreams*. The above therefore makes you your own prophet in dreams. Now let us deal with visions.

There are three types of visions in the Bible. We will deal with the lowest to the highest type of vision and from the highest to the lowest type of revelation. The spiritual vision, the trance, and the open vision. Since we are dealing with the visions of the night (in dreams) we can confidently point out that the visions of the night are the fourth type. In hindsight do recall that any type of vision you see can only fall into three categories, the word of wisdom, and the word of knowledge or the discerning of spirits as discussed above. Thus:

Spiritual Vision: This is any vision you see in your spirit with your eyes closed. For many, it occurs during prayer. It is the lowest type of vision yet the highest type of revelation.

> *As Saul was coming near the city of Damascus, a light from heaven suddenly flashed around him. He fell to the ground and heard a voice say to him, "Saul! Saul! Why are you persecuting me?" Saul asked, "Who are you, sir?" The person replied, "I'm Jesus, the one you're persecuting. Get up! Go into the city, and you'll be told what you should do." Meanwhile, the men traveling with him*

were speechless. They heard the voice but didn't see anyone. Saul was helped up from the ground. When he opened his eyes, he was blind. So his companions led him into Damascus. (Acts 9:3-8)

Trance: This is the second type of vision. When one falls into a trance his physical senses are momentarily suspended. It is a place where one feels as if unconscious meanwhile conscious but of the realm of the spirit. That individual is not conscious of self, time, and matter but captured in the moment of the vision. Acts 10:10 GW, *"He became hungry and wanted to eat. While the food was being prepared, he fell into a trance."* A trance is not limited to a deep sleep type of experience it can also occur with your eyes wide open, Num. 24:16 GW, *"This is the message of the one who hears the words of God, receives knowledge from the Most High, has a vision from the Almighty, and falls into a trance with his eyes open."*

Open Vision: This is any type of vision seen with eyes wide open. This is the highest type of vision but the lowest type of revelation.

> *Samuel took a flask of olive oil, poured it on Saul's head, kissed him, and said, "The LORD has anointed you to be the ruler of his people Israel. You will rule his people and save them from all their enemies. This will be the sign that the LORD has anointed you to be ruler of his people. When you leave me today, two men will be at Rachel's grave on the border of Benjamin at Zelzah. They'll tell you, 'We've found the donkeys you went looking for. Your father no longer cares about them. Instead, he's worried about you. He keeps asking, "What can I do to find my son?"' Keep going until you come to the oak tree at Tabor. There you will find three men on their way to worship God at Bethel: One will be carrying three young goats, one will be carrying*

three loaves of bread, and one will be carrying a full wineskin. They will greet you and give you two loaves of bread, which you should accept from them. After that, you will come to the hill of God, where the Philistines have a military post. When you arrive at the city, you will meet a group of prophets prophesying as they come from the worship site. They will be led by men playing a harp, a tambourine, a flute, and a lyre. Then the LORD'S Spirit will come over you. You will be a different person while you prophesy with them. When these signs happen to you, do what you must, because God is with you. Go ahead of me to Gilgal. Then I will come to sacrifice burnt offerings and make fellowship offerings. Wait seven days until I come to tell you what to do." (1 Sam. 10:1-8 GW).

Since we have laid out the three types of visions we will now deal with the Visions of the night.

Visions of the night: This type of vision occurs during one's deep sleep. At times you will hardly know whether it was a dream or vision except by the context. One particular Old Testament prophet who was consistently used in this area was Daniel. Here is one of his visions quoted below:

Dan. 7:2 KJV, *"Daniel spake and said, I saw in my vision by night, and, behold, the four winds of the heaven strove upon the great sea."*

In this vision Daniel saw four animals, the first was a lion with wings, the second animal was a bear raised on its side, the third was a leopard with four wings and the fourth animal is described as terrible and fearful having large iron teeth. This was a vision of the night. How do we know that? By Daniel dreaming a dream he is not part of or simply put he wasn't the subject of the dream. But if you be the subject the dream is mainly about you. If you are not the subject then the dream points to something other than you. The subject of Daniel's dream is the four animals. This dream was a word of wisdom in that God was revealing His plans and purposes to Daniel.

We know by the context that these animals signified four kingdoms. And in chapter 8 two of these kingdoms are explained to be Medo-Persia and Greece. In dreams and visions, we interpret a prop or a characteristic in the context of the dream to get to the underlying meaning. Here the characteristics and wings of the lion represented the kingdom of Babylon that was the ruling empire in Daniel's time. The bear represented the characteristics of the aggressive kingdom of the Medo-Persians ruled by Cyrus the great which was to come. And the bear Daniel saw was foreshadowing the third powerful empire which would arise 250 years after Daniel. It was swift and agile in conquering. The fourth animal Daniel saw represented the last and the most powerful kingdom that is still to come before the Second Coming of Christ. See my book The Prophecy.

Dan. 8:27 GW, "I, Daniel, was exhausted and sick for days. Then I got up and worked for the king. The vision horrified me because I couldn't understand it."

In this particular vision, Daniel's vision of the night (chapter 8) was narrowed to only two empires. Medo-Persia and Greece's frequent clashes and wars. Daniel again was not the subject of the dream but the observer.

How to distinguish visions of the night? A vision is separate from a dream with characteristics such as:

- Dreaming looking through a house's backyard: this means you are seeing into your family's past, or to the past of the person the house belongs to.
- Dreaming yourself in a car looking through the rearview mirror.

- Dreaming yourself observing an incident from a mountain, aerial view position, or looking through a window or watching television, etc.
- Dreaming yourself inside someone else's living room: this means you are seeing what is presently happening in that person's life.
- Dreaming yourself in someone's bedroom: this means you are being shown the issues or secret things of the heart of the person the bedroom belongs to.
- Dreaming of someone's house concerns matters of that person's life or situation.
- Dreaming someone's clothes that concerns that individuals' actions.

Notice that you are the observer. In this case, someone else or a particular group or nation is the subject of the dream other than yourself. It is also possible for a dream to address a message to two people. This becomes a vision type of a dream to the other individual you dreamt alongside you. A good example is my dream shared in the Preface. To me, that was a dream but to my Pastor, it was a vision. God revealing his future walk of faith and that he was to be later blessed with a son. After making this dream known to him, he was reassured as he expressed his longing for a son since he had two daughters. In short, when a dream's subject, item, clothes, car, house, keys (principles), shoes belong to someone else that dream is a vision that God has entrusted to you to tell the individual that he or she may know where they stand in God's plan, purpose, and destiny entrusted to them. After telling the individual it is important that you pray for the person. There is a high blessing when we pray for others than when we pray for ourselves. The Kingdom of God is founded on love and unselfishness. Prayer is the only powerful force that changes events on earth where man's ability is limited.

Chapter 7

ANGELS AND DREAMS

Angels play an integral part in dreams. They have the power to give us dreams. This explains why we have to differentiate between diabolic and divine dreams. The devil can create dreams as much as the angels of God can.

> *With disturbing thoughts from visions in the night, when deep sleep falls on people, fear and trembling came over me, and all my bones shook. A spirit passed in front of me. It made my hair stand on end. Something stood there. I couldn't tell what it was. A vague image was in front of my eyes. I heard a soft voice: Can any mortal be righteous to God? Can any human being be pure to his maker?' "You see, God doesn't trust his own servants, and he accuses his angels of making mistakes. How much more will he accuse those who live in clay houses that have their foundation in the dust. Those houses can be crushed quicker than a moth! From morning to evening, they are shattered. They will disappear forever without anyone paying attention. Haven't the ropes of their tent been loosened? Won't they die without wisdom?* (Job 4:13-21GW).

Eliphaz alluded to this vision of the night he once had to Job and his other friends. In this vision of the night, a fallen angel appeared condemning man and complaining about God. This is one of the many proofs you shall see as we explore angels using dreams to communicate to men. Demonic dreams create oppression for anyone that entertains them.

Hearing God's voice in Dreams

Col. 1:16 KJV, *"For by him were all things created, that are in heaven, and that are in earth, visible and invisible, whether they be thrones, or dominions, or principalities, or powers: all things were created by him, and for him."* In the revelation God gave to Paul we find four ranks of angels. This is not to be confused with the one of Ephesians 6:12 which is a diabolic hierarchy of fallen angels and demons. The one of Colossians is the hierarchy of angels that still serve God. Eph. 3:10 GW, *"To the intent that now unto the principalities and powers in heavenly places might be known by the church the manifold wisdom of God."* Ephesians 1:21 KJV, *"Far above all principality, and power, and might, and dominion, and every name that is named, not only in this world but also in that which is to come."* In Ephesians, there is another rank mentioned as Might which is left out in Colossians. And in Colossians, there is another rank mentioned as Thrones which is left out in Ephesians.

1. Principalities
2. Powers
3. Might (Dunamis)
4. Dominions
5. Thrones

The order is not mainly important since the subject of the context is Christ. We are well aware that there are different angelic departments we won't necessarily deal with them for this study we will focus on matters in proximity or correlating to dreams. The word Thrones can also be translated as Kings and Dominions as Lordships. Between these two the order is distinguishable, the first and higher is Thrones and then follows suit the Dominions. These are the angelic beings that are responsible for dreams, ideas, and the rise of great leaders. Dominions are responsible for godly policies, divine strategies, godly governance, etc. Together these hierarchies are responsible for family wellbeing, inventions, civilization, and great leadership. Should the Church realize what is at its disposal many desert countries would be flooded with rivers of inventions.

Hearing God's voice in Dreams

When Jesus was born according to the Gospel of Matthew an angel appeared to Joseph in a dream instructing him to take the baby and his mother and flee to Egypt (chapter 2:13).

Later, the same angel appeared again to Joseph in Egypt with news that they who sought to kill the child are dead he should go back to the land of Israel (vs. 19-21). This was not the Angel of the Lord that had appeared countless times in the Old Testament. The Angel of the Lord in the Old Testament was Christ in pre-incarnation. We know by what the Angel said to Abraham when he was about to sacrifice Isaac on that mountain, Gen. 22:15-17 KJV, *"And the angel of the LORD called unto Abraham out of heaven the second time, And said,* **By myself have I sworn**, *saith the LORD, for because thou hast done this thing, and hast not withheld thy son, thine only son. That in blessing I will bless thee, and in multiplying I will multiply thy seed..."* And in the book of Hebrews that Angel is explained to be God Himself. Heb. 6:13-14 KJV, *"For when God made promise to Abraham, because he could swear by no greater, he sware by himself, Saying, Surely blessing I will bless thee, and multiplying I will multiply thee."*

The angel in Matthew could not be this angel for the Angel of the Lord in the Old Testament was God and that God was wrapped up in the arms of Mary. This was just a normal angel. Justifying the fact that any normal angel can form dreams. Rightfully in many translations, the Angel of the Lord in the Old Testament has the definite article 'the' while the angel that appears throughout the New Testament has the indefinite article 'an' angel of the Lord in translations like Darby, American Standard Version, Contemporary English Version, Douay Rheims Bible, etc. But the King James Bible tends to fail in this differentiating, see verses like Mat. 2:13, 19, Lk. 2:9, Acts 5:19, 8:26, 12:7.

Nebuchadnezzar had a second dream; in it, he saw a huge and tall tree that reached heaven. It was in the center of the earth and could be seen from anywhere on earth. It was richly covered with leaves, stacked with fruits, abundant that they could feed nations. The beasts of the field found shade under it, the birds of the heavens decked its branches and every living thing found sustenance from the tree (Dan. 4:4-12). Dan. 4:13 Darby, *"I saw in the visions of my head upon my bed, and behold, a watcher and a holy one came down from the heavens."* The word watcher in this portion is derived from the Chaldean word 'ur' meaning a watcher. A watcher is a sentinel, a guardian. God has set some angels to be guardians over our lives (see Psa. 91:11-12) and some to be guardians over creation (see Rev. 16:5). You can substitute the word watchers with angels.

> *He shouted, 'Cut down the oak tree! Cut off its branches! Strip off its leaves! Scatter its fruit! Make the animals under it run away, and make the birds fly from its branches. But leave the stump and its roots in the ground. Secure it with an iron and bronze chain in the grass in the field. Let it get wet with the dew from the sky. And let it get its share of the plants on the ground with the animals. Let its human mind be changed, and give it the mind of an animal. Let it remain like this for seven time periods. The guardians/angels have announced this decision. The holy ones/angels have announced this so that every living creature will know that the Most High has power over human kingdoms. He gives them to whomever he wishes. He can place the lowest of people in charge of them.'* (Dan. 4:14-17 GW, Emphasis Added)

Notice, verse 13 draws our attention to Nebuchadnezzar seeing a particular angel in his dream coming down from heaven. And crying out *cut down the tree, cut off its branches, fruits and scatter its fruits*. Then verse 17 states this decree is by the angels or call it watchers. CEV, puts it, *"This punishment is given at the command of the holy angels."* God's Word translation, *"The guardians have announced this decision."* Therefore, this was a decision decided by a special inner circle of angels.

These angels (watchers) seem to hold a special position in the angelic realm. Concerning the decree being decided by the watchers, this was made known to Nebuchadnezzar in the dream while he only saw one watcher coming down from heaven. We know through the text and the ways and dealings of God that the one watcher who released the decree, a decree from a council of watchers must be the leader in this class of angelic beings. The text identifies the decision coming from angelic beings, not God.

Because they acted in God's Word and within His standards of righteousness thus it is the work of God. *"This is the meaning, Your Majesty. The Most High has decided to apply it to you, Your Majesty."* Vs 24. Contrary to what we thought. We always assumed angels did little thinking on their own, everything they did was what God told them. That is not true, God holds angels responsible as much as he holds men responsible. They have a soul (mind, will, and emotions). That is why some chose to rebel against God. And they have higher intelligence and wisdom than fallen men. 2 Sam. 14:17 Holman Christian Standard Bible, *"Your servant thought: May the word of my lord the king bring relief, for my lord the king is able to discern the good and the bad like the Angel of God. May the LORD your God be with you."* It is only the New Creation that has the highest type of wisdom, the wisdom of Christ (1 Cor. 1:30).

The watcher continued that the tree should be hewn down but the stump to remain on its roots to the ground. Dan. 4:16 Darby, *"Let his heart be changed from man's, and let a beast's heart be given unto him; and let seven times pass over him."* By this portion, we get to see that this is not about a literal tree because the watcher shifts from the tree to addressing a man using an analogy of a tree, *"Let his heart be changed from a man's and he be given a beast's heart."* A tree has no human mind nor a human heart. Nebuchadnezzar summoned all the astrologers, scribes, magicians, and Chaldeans but none could make the dream known to the king until Daniel was summoned. Daniel after being quiet for an hour revealed the interpretation of the dream to the king. That the watchers had decided to cut Nebuchadnezzar from his kingdom to live with the beasts of the field but his kingdom will not be stripped away from him as the stump of the tree and its roots remained on the ground in his dream.

This happened after 12 months, see verses 28 to 33. The purpose of this decision by the watchers was to humble Nebuchadnezzar because his heart had turned prideful and reveal to him that God is the only ultimate King and God of all honor and glory and He gives kingdoms to whomsoever He wills, Dan. 4:30-31 GW, *"The king thought, "Look how great Babylon is! I built the royal palace by my own impressive power and for my glorious honor." Before the words came out of his mouth, a voice said from heaven,* **"King Nebuchadnezzar, listen to this: The kingdom has been taken from you."** This voice was from the watcher he had seen in his dream. God would have addressed him as Nebuchadnezzar without reference to his title 'king.' 2 Pet. 2:10-11 GW, *"but chiefly them that walk after the flesh in the lust of defilement, and despise dominion. Daring, self-willed, they tremble not to rail at dignities: whereas angels, though greater in might and power, bring not a railing judgment against them before the Lord."*

For seven years Nebuchadnezzar was forced to live like a beast of the field, he ate grass, his body was bathed by the dew of heaven, his nails grew like birds' claws and his hair grew larger than eagle's feathers. After seven years he was restored to his understanding and he praised and glorified God. This also brings us back to chapter 3, *what are Dreams Most About*? And where we intimated in the previous chapters, *"In a dream, a prophetic vision at night, when people fall into a deep sleep, when they sleep on their beds, ... He warns them to turn away from doing wrong and to stop being arrogant."* Job 33:15 & 17 GW.

The angel in my dream

Hearing God's voice in Dreams

In the year 2012, I had a dream where I encountered an angel. This dream forever changed the course of my ministry. It was the early morning hours of the Good Friday of the 13th of April. Before this dream, I had an intense hunger for the Word of God since 2009. On an average Saturday, I'd spend an average of 7 to 8 hours studying the Word without having breakfast or going for a bath. After all that I still had more thirst to know God more through His Word.

On that Good Friday early hours, I had a dream, in this dream, I saw a Pastor who according to the dream was my mentor and leader, someone I know. His eyes were terrifying and he had an aura of dignity around him and looked solemn. Right there in the dream, I had a knowing without a doubt that I am standing before an angel sent from heaven to me. This angel spoke in an authoritative deep voice, he said, *"I will lay hands on you and upon you will come the spirit of Wisdom, Understanding, and Knowledge of the Scriptures."* As soon as he laid his hands on me, one was placed on my chest and the other was on my back, I fell face ward to the ground. I then woke up from the dream and understood that that was an impartation from God through an angel.

Early that morning my pastor, James Chirinda tried contacting me to start the conference with ministering. There was a sudden change in speakers. I missed all the calls as a result of oversleeping due to tiredness. My youth leader knocked on my door, it was a cold morning around 8 am this was before I became a youth leader in the House of Prayer. She was sent with a message that I should prepare I will be ministering that morning. The pressure felt high for me since we were in collaboration with Gateway Ministries from Pretoria north of Johannesburg. Our visitors were to arrive that early morning. I did not get time to pray in the morning as usual due to oversleeping. I am oddly a slow preparer, and it's one of the things my wife usually scolds me for. I had not enough time to prepare a sermon too. Upon being at church during the worship service I had laid in my spirit Isaiah 6 and the message was supposed to be about the Glory of God. Our church was packed to capacity and to overflowing. I stood to minister; I had never felt the way I felt that day. It was the beginning of something new in my ministry. It was the anointing of ministering. In the middle of the sermon, the anointing of preaching took over.

I remember people on their feet, some with tears on their eyes, and in the front seat brother Lebo one of our visitors and the youth leader of Gateway Ministries was shivering as he buried his head in his thighs and a few others too were shaking. Most asked me during the intermission of the morning service before the second service what had happened to me. I could not explain but I knew it was the dream. Following that day to now my way of seeing and interpreting Scriptures had been revolutionized. This has impacted my life to some great degree including some of our church members.

"I came to give you skill to interpret visions"

Can angels give us wisdom and understanding or skill to interpret visions? The answer is an undeniable yes. Let's look through the Scriptures to find our answer.

The Lord seeks a constant reliance and relationship from us. We will never attain a level where we are sufficed with Him. A good example here is Daniel. I want you to observe his pattern in his dream interpretation career. Daniel found himself and his kind in an awkward position when king Nebuchadnezzar was furious to annihilate the wise men of Babylon due to their failure in telling him his dream and also interpreting the dream a task never before demanded by any king (see Dan. 2). While the guards were trying to find Daniel and his friends, famously known as Shadrach, Meshach, and Abednego.

These four had been escalated to the position of wise men of Babylon because of their wisdom and intelligence as explained in the first chapter of Daniel. When the guards found them. They were enlightened to the situation at hand. Daniel personally approached the king seeking time to finding the dream interpretation. The king out of his mercy granted them time. This happens to be the first encounter of Daniel in regards to dream interpretation. Again observe the order especially if you are to interpret dreams. This will be the order we will outline in the chapter on dream interpretation.

In chapter 1 of the book of Daniel God rewarded Daniel and his friends with attractiveness, favor, wisdom, and knowledge to understanding all the literature and sciences of Babylon. And specifically to Daniel who was the leader of the group God gave him the understanding of all kinds of visions and dreams (vs.17b). In chapter 2 when Nebuchadnezzar the king had a dream, he did not tell it to anyone but summoned all the wise men, astrologers, and magicians of Babylon.

The king demanded they tell him the dream and the interpretation. He believed if he would tell them the dream anyone of them might lie of the interpretation. This was an impossible task as the king reverted to annihilating all of them from the land. When Daniel and his friends heard asked for time to search out the matter of the king. That same night the dream was revealed to Daniel and its interpretation in the vision of the night. Dan. 2:19 CEV, *"In a vision one night, Daniel was shown the dream and its meaning. Then he praised the God who rules from heaven."* In this aspect I want you to deliberately observe that Daniel did no dream interpretation on his own but he was shown the dream and the interpretation. All he did was to just trust in the Lord, and then he dreamt the dream, and also received the interpretation, and then woke up to tell the king.

In many dreams interpretation books this is the one aspect left out, dependence upon God for dreams and visions interpretation. Many books only focus on the skill aspect there is nothing wrong with that but there is a thin line between interpretation and inspiration. Dream interpretation usually takes 80% of skill and 20% of inspiration. So we need both. When you are starting in this wonderful journey of dreams interpretation like Daniel the Lord will supernaturally help you in finding the right meaning of dreams but as you grow the Lord expects that experience to grow to a skill of course that does not mean the skill rules out God from dreams interpretation. God is the true revealer of mysteries both Daniel and Joseph understood this at face value. Gen. 41:16 CEV, *"Your Majesty," Joseph answered, "I can't do it myself, but God can give a good meaning to your dreams."*

Let us now skip to chapter 9 of Daniel. This was over 45 years since chapter 1. Daniel had been undoubtedly having success in the interpretation of his dreams and of others that we cannot dispute, for a good example look into chapter four, seven, and eight. Daniel had quite some experience for over four decades and a half of dreams interpretation but still, he had to learn to trust more on God in this journey of dreams interpretation. In chapter 9 he seems to have had a bit of confusion somehow in his career. For nearly 50 years Daniel and his kind were in captivity in the land of Babylon. In his knowledge of the Scriptures, he calls into account the fact that it is written that after 70 years God would release his people from Babylon and return them to their land.

Out of godly concern and zeal, Daniel supplicates to God according to that promise. There are times even the best of us are shaken and wonder if the promises made upon our lives will ever be fulfilled. As occasionally seen in Scriptures God does strengthen us through His angels in our times of weaknesses. Look at what the angel said to Daniel upon reaching him, *"And he informed me, and talked with me, and said, O Daniel, I am now come forth to give thee skill and understanding."* Dan. 9:22 KJV. Gabriel came to give Daniel one of the two most important aspects of dreams and visions interpretation: 1. Skill and 2. Understanding. What he had gained in chapter 1 about 45 years ago will not carry him for the remaining years ahead. He needed the skill to understand the deepest dreams and visions that were coming ahead. After this, we see the most descriptive, accurate, and detailed prophecy in Scriptures of the future events Daniel foresaw that have caused some Bible commentators to doubt Daniel's books dating with such claims that it might have been written after all the events had happened, events that were to transpire after the third empire had taken over the known worlds, the Grecian empire of Alexander the Great, the prophecy written in chapter 11. Details concerning his (Alexander the Great's) four generals, the dividing of his kingdom. The wars between its kings and dynasties to the type of the antichrist, Antiochus Epiphanes. I deal with the details of Daniel 11 in the 13th chapter of my book the Prophecy.

There we have it, according to the above segment angels can give us the skill to understanding and interpret dreams as seen in the quoted excerpt from the book of Daniel when the angel Gabriel came to Daniel he explicitly told him he came to give him the skill and understanding. I call you to the remembrance of what I had mentioned at the beginning of this chapter that Thrones are angels responsible for dreams, ideas, and the raising of leaders. Gabriel in this instance is an angel falling in the rank of Thrones, he holds a special high rank in the angelic realm. Dan. 7:2-3 GW, *"In my visions at night I, Daniel, saw the four winds of heaven stirring up the Mediterranean Sea. Four large animals, each one different from the others, came out of the sea."*

The four winds of heaven stirring the Mediterranean Sea and four beasts coming out of the sea imply heaven's agenda and power behind the rising of the four empires that will dominate till the Lord comes. Connect this with our opening segment of this chapter concerning the watchers, the guardian angels that were responsible for the establishment of King Nebuchadnezzar in Babylon. These types of angels and all other angels on earth are all responsible for helping us the Saints bring righteousness to the earth and the knowledge of God. They are also our servants in this Kingdom we are in, Heb. 1:14 KJV, *"Are they not all ministering spirits, sent forth to minister for them who shall be heirs of salvation?"*

Hearing God's voice in Dreams

I am more convinced that as the Church we are yet to see greater angelic activity in our life such as has not been seen beginning from the dreams realm. Angels were so active in the early church that disciples were admonished in how they treat strangers. Heb. 13:2 GW, *"Don't forget to show hospitality to believers you don't know. By doing this some believers have shown hospitality to angels without being aware of it."* The latter glory (our church age) shall be greater than the former (early church age), see Hag. 2:9.

Patron Angels

"That God Most High gave land to every nation. He assigned a guardian angel to each of them." (Deu. 32:8 CEV).

The above verse is of great dispute, other versions like the King James Version have it, *"When the most High divided to the nations their inheritance, when he separated the sons of Adam, he set the bounds of the people according to the number of the children of Israel."* When it goes as God separating the sons of Adam which is the whole human race and setting the bounds according to the children of Israel it brings confusion.

Wherever there is confusion there is a deception. The confusion springs from the two words 'children of Israel, when in Hebrew it's children 'bane' meaning Sons, not children, and the word Israel Hebrew rightfully 'El' meaning God. This then should be the Sons of God *'Ben ha Eli.'* The same words in Genesis 6:1, Job 1:6, 2:1 which refers to angels, they are called the Sons of God because of the Hebrew concept of their being God's direct creation. Versions that have it as angels it's the Septuagint, Contemporary English Version, English Standard Version, and New American Bible Revised Edition. The NET Bible second edition has it, *"...according to the number of the heavenly assembly."* God did not set the bounds of the people according to the number of the children of Israel. Instead, it makes sense when it's translated as God setting bounds according to the Sons of God (angels) because every nation under the sun has a tutelary angel, angels which are attributed as Princes over nations. Gabriel related being withstood by the Prince of Persia on his way to Daniel while carrying Daniel's answer from God (Dan. 10:12-13). It should be an accepted belief that every nation has a guardian or Prince angel over it. For the nation of Israel, it's Michael the Chief Commander of Heaven's Army. *"At that time Michael, the great prince who watches over your people, will arise. There will be a time of distress unlike any other from the nation's beginning up to that time. But at that time your own people, all those whose names are found written in the book will escape."* Dan. 12:1 NET2.

These guardian angels wrestle alongside us against the forces of darkness. We empower them through our prayers and confessions of the Word of God. They are coworkers with us to bringing the Kingdom of God into a visible manifestation to this earth. Be careful therefore to not to pray or worship created beings. We are called to worship the creator. In the New Testament, angels are serving us the heirs of Salvation (Heb. 1:14). They are beneath us we are at the God class. As seen above these angels do bring us dreams to see where we are in God's timeline and where we are headed. It would change our lives if we would see that 90% of activities in this world are driven by unseen forces, I submit the political arenas, financial institutions, economic booms and busts, wars you name them. We need to awaken to the realities of the spiritual realm that includes dreams.

The excerpt below I have added to this chapter because of its scriptural basis. The Word of God in our lives should be the basis of how we measure every experience not experiences to dictate how we interpret the Word.

Pastor Joe Sweet shared an experience Bob Jones had when he died and went before the Lord in 1975. He said he was just outside of heaven. The Lord stood outside there were three people that died ahead of him. They were about to go into heaven. One was an eleven-year-old girl, another one was a lady in her nineties, another was a black lady who had been an evangelist on earth and

Bob had his angel standing with him and the angel was explaining to him what he was seeing. He relates that he saw each person as they approached the Lord, the Lord asked them, and *"Did you learn to love?"* he said no one can lie in the Lord's presence. He said the first lady, the lady in her nineties she did love the Lord but she did not walk in love before the people. She became bitter. She hung her head in shame and wept, she said, *"No, Lord only you. I only loved You. I was bitter."*

Bob was made to know that she had no rewards but she missed hell (see my book The Prophecy). He was also made to know that she barely made it to heaven. He says the Lord wiped away her tears, kissed her on the forehead, and pulled her to himself. He said I was made to understand the Scripture that says Jesus is the door, He was. He pulled her right through into His heart she went right through Him into heaven. The next one was the eleven-year-old girl and Bob was told by the angel that was with him, he said, *"This girl at eleven years old has already amassed great rewards. The last four years of her life she spent on her sickbed she had leukemia or something like that.* He said, *"she was a believer since a little girl she loved God and she never gave in to self-pity instead she spent all those hours confined to her bed not saying why can't I play why am I not healed* (this does not mean we have to tolerate sickness.

Jesus has paid the price for our healing. But just because a believer dies from sickness it does not make them less of a Christian). She spent all those hours interceding for other people to be saved and drawn close to God. And the angel said, *"She already has great reward in heaven."* The Lord asked her, *"Did you learn to love?"* He kissed her and bowed her head. The next lady was a black lady, she had a dozen angels with her. Bob asked his angel, *"Why does she have more angels than the rest of us?"* Because when you go the angel that's assigned to you on earth goes to heaven with you. The angels that are with you on earth are hoping that you will obey God because they get to help you when you do God's will and when you out of God's will they don't. They are only sent to help you do

Hearing God's voice in Dreams

the will of God. So, your angels are wanting to get to heaven and get to have a testimony, that's what Bob was told. They want to have a testimony, *"We did well on the earth, we helped so and so. They gave their lives to God and we worked with them."* They don't want to just say, *"Yeah, they were rebelling and all the time we kept them from dying and car accidents."*

The more we obey God the happier angels are. The angel answered Bob, *"She was an evangelist, and she'd spend hours praying for people to be saved. The more she would pray for people to be saved in her meetings these angels would go out and help gather the people in. They would influence the people to come to the meeting as they would get saved."* Bob said the Lord asked her, *"Did you learn to love?"* he said she threw her head back and belly laughed she said, *"I learned to love."*

How to identify angels in dreams?

As in Bible time's angels or the Holy Spirit would be revealed as a faceless person:

> *a man found him wandering around in the open country. "What are you looking for?" the man asked. Joseph replied, "I'm looking for my brothers. Please tell me where they're taking care of their flocks." The man said, "They moved on from here. I heard them say, 'Let's go to Dothan.'" So Joseph went after his brothers and found them at Dothan.* (Gen. 37:15-17 GW)

Should you dream someone you know or felt acquainted to in a dream but can't make up his face or who the person was, that was an angel in your dream. Many times we dream of embarking on a long journey with someone we feel comfortable with and somewhat we may call a close companion in the dream. But when we wake up, we can't know who it was, that was an angel in your dream. God is letting you know that in this journey you are embarking on or whatever you seem to be facing in your life you are not alone He has assigned a protector and guardian for you.

There is a thin line between an angel and the Holy Spirit in your dreams. Many times, you might think it's an angel when it is the Holy Spirit. You know it is the Holy Spirit when you felt like the person was your friend in the dream but after waking up you could not remember his face. In this aspect, it has to be a male as also is the aspect of an angel. We normally come across male angels according to the Scriptures. Pro. 18:24 KJV, *"A man that hath friends must shew himself friendly: and there is a friend that sticketh closer than a brother."*

In the book of Ruth, we have a type of the Holy Spirit. Ruth was a type of a gentile bride, the Church, Naomi represents her people, Israel, and Boaz a type of Jesus Christ. As much as the context is important in the text so is context important in dreams. Below is the type of the Holy Spirit in the book of Ruth:

> *Boaz asked the young man in charge of his reapers, "Who is this young woman?" The young man answered, "She's a young Moabite woman who came back with Naomi from the country of Moab. She said, 'Please let me gather grain. I will only gather among the bundles behind the reapers.' So she came here and has been on her feet from daybreak until now. She just sat down this minute in the shelter."* (Rut. 2:5-7 GW).

The above portion of Scripture mentions a servant who is the overlord of servants. That cannot be a type for an angel but the type of the Holy Spirit. He is the One that has introduced Ruth, you the believer to Christ.

Chapter 8

HOW DREAMS HAVE SHAPED THE WORLD

The first African King who saw white missionaries in a dream

The Swati king, Sobhuza I, also known as Somhlolo, one night shortly before his death in 1836. In the morning he summoned his councilors and explained to them that white-skinned people with hair like the tails of cattle will arrive in his country bringing with them Umculu (scroll) and Indilinga (a round piece of metal, coin). The book he saw was taken to represent the Bible and the coin money.

He warned his people and advised them that they are to never harm these people for if they split a drop of white man's blood their country would be destroyed and they would disappear as a nation. The missionaries arrived in 1844.

Apostle Nicholas B. H Bhengu, a vision that shook South Africa

Apostle Bhengu a man led strongly by God in dreams and visions, was an evangelist, a teacher of the Word, and a pastor. Through his ministry, a very large congregation was built up in the Eastern Cape, KwaZulu-Natal, and the rest of South Africa together with the neighboring countries the Assemblies of God.

Like any other general of the faith, his story also has a beginning. How he started was of a dream where he saw two birds sit on his shoulders. One asked the other, "Should we give him?" The second bird answered, "Yes because he has conquered these three things, the pride of life, the love of money, and the skirt (the love of women)." In 1932 he went to America seeking funding for his vision of bringing "Africa back to God from Cape to Cairo" as it would be his famous slogan. It is there where he co-partnered with a white woman to preaching the gospel. His preaching amassed crowds, they'd make converts out of the crowds. The story goes on how the woman would take over and draw the crowds to her ministry which wasn't part of their plan. At some point Apostle Bhengu frustrated and dissatisfied that the woman is stealing his people he decided to split and form his ministry.

In a dream of the night he dreamt chopping a stem of a missive tree and its branches, surprisingly blood came out, shocked at the ordeal he heard a voice warning him, "You do not have people that belong to you. Leave the people and go start alone." He left them and went on preaching and gained new converts. On another account while obsessed with finding funding in the United States he received a vision not sure if it was a dream, he saw barefoot women, smoking long and thin pipes with money stuck on their large white kerchiefs. And the Lord spoke to him, "This is where your money is." He knew right there that the money he was looking for, for his ministry was in the "Xhosa land," the women of Eastern Cape of South Africa could finance the vision. About 1945 he traveled to Port Elizabeth. His little son died on the way he buried him in a box of tomatoes. He preached in a garage with no chairs, people sat on crates. His great following came from the Methodist in which he incorporated their hymn books into his ministry.

In 1950 he went to East London where he preached the paint off the walls. It was to be remembered as the most anointed sermon. Known for his humility he went on saying, "I don't own it, this is God's thing." Today, in South Africa the Assemblies of God remains the biggest mainstream denomination.

Julius Caesar's wife's dream

Before Julius Caesar was assassinated Calpurnia his wife dreamt a statue of Caesar was flowing with blood as many Romans washed their hands in that blood. Despite the many warnings Julius Caesar received he still went headlong with his decision on to the Theatre of Pompey.

Hearing God's voice in Dreams

It was on March the 15th of 44 B.C during a meeting of the Senate at the Theatre of Pompey in Rome that the senators stabbed Julius Caesar 23 times, he fell dead at the foot of the statue of his old enemy Pompey. The senators expressed fear over Caesar as they thought that Caesar's unprecedented concentration of power during his dictatorship was undermining the Roman Republic. With a total of 60 senates as part of the conspiracy. This was led by Marcus Brutus, Gaius Cassius, and Decimus Brutus. The conspirators hoped his death would revive the old spirit of Rome. Consequently, after the death of Caesar, the conspirators failed to restore the institutions of Rome. The Roman citizens became increasingly hostile. The conspirators fled Rome and all ultimately met their end. The implications of his assassination led to the Liberator's civil war and the Principate period of the Roman Empire.

The Apollo 13 Malfunction

On April 13, 1970, three astronauts Jimmy Lovell, Fred Haise, and Jack Swigert were sent on a space mission to the moon on a spacecraft named Apollo 13. Three days just before the launch Jimmy Lovell's wife, Marilyn Lovell dreamt her husband sucked out through an open door of their spacecraft into outer space. While on the space mission Apollo 13 had a malfunction caused by an explosion and rupture of the oxygen tank no.2. The explosion instigated a rupture in no.1 oxygen tank which cost the ship a rapid loss of oxygen. The three astronauts had to huddle in an undamaged lunar module which was a spacecraft designed for two men to land on the moon.

The men had to only power the essential systems of the spacecraft to save energy, they were exposed to colds. The whole world stood with their families in prayer hoping for their safe return, with the help of Mission Control after four days the men safely landed back to earth.

President Abraham Lincoln

Hearing God's voice in Dreams

He went on being a lawyer and pursued politics failing over ten times and having lost his wife became a President in 1860-1865. He is the first person to come against the slavery system in the United States. Facing opposition from the fellow congressman, family, friends and mostly the northern part of the continent persevered until he broke the slavery system. He was then assassinated. Agreeably America's best all-time president dreamt of his assassination in the dream he could hear subdued sobs of several people weeping he went from room to room and each time he found no living person in the rooms he kept on until he arrived in the east room in the white house he came upon his corpse according to the account it is said that he heard a guard saying the president had been assassinated he removed the cloth covering the corpse he realized it was him this was days before the assassination happened.

Dr. Benjamin Carson

At the University of Michigan Medical School, he focused on reading alone and skipping lectures. During his last examination period, he struggled to balance a chemical equation that he decided to work on it most of the night before his exam. He fell asleep and dreamt his professor scribing the right answer on a blackboard. He looked at the answer and woke up from his dream. The following day, which would be his exam day, on the paper the equation appeared; he remembered the answer and wrote it while his fellow students struggled. He made something of about 97 or 98 percent on his last exams. From that time on he went on to believe in miracles, which he related to his interviewer when asked what made him think he was qualified for the post offered since many other brilliant young men also applied for it.

Among his achievements as a surgeon was the separation of conjoined twins in 1987, here is where he made medical history with an operation to separate a pair of Siamese twins. The Binder twins were joined together at the back of the head. Operations to separate twins joined in this way had always failed, resulting in the death of one or both of the infants. The operation undertook 22 hours. In the end, the twins were successfully separated and continued surviving independently. Other surgical innovations included the first intra-uterine procedure to relieve the pressure of the brain of a hydrocephalic fetal twin and a hemispherectomy for an infant suffering from uncontrollable seizures having half of the brain removed. This stops the seizures and the remaining half of the brain compensates for the missing hemisphere. He was recognized for his achievements in 2008 by President George W. Bush with the Presidential Medal of Freedom, this is the nation's highest civilian honor.

Solomon's Source of Wisdom

Solomon the son of King David succeeded his father to the throne. After his inauguration, he summoned the elders of his people and ascended to a high place in Gibeon. He offered one thousand sacrifices on the altar of the high place. God appeared to him in a dream asking what He should do for him. Solomon asked the Lord to give him wisdom. The Lord granted him wisdom and riches as well (2 Chr. 1:1-11).

Here was an ancient king who spoke three thousand proverbs and had written one thousand and five songs (1 Ki. 4:32). His book, the book of Proverbs is widely popular among circular and Christian circles for its timely wisdom in matters of character, leadership, and finances. He reigned for forty years and there was no war at all during his days. He built the House of the Lord for thirteen years. He overlaid it inside with gold (1 Ki. 6:2 &21). Between three years and four years ago it was estimated that Solomon's gold inside the Temple weighed over $200 billion.

> *"The king also made a large ivory throne and covered it with fine gold. Six steps led to the throne. Carved into the back of the throne was a calf's head. There were armrests on both sides of the seat. Two lions stood beside the armrests. Twelve lions stood on six*

steps, one on each side. Nothing like this had been made for any other kingdom." (1 Ki. 10:18-20 GW)

"The king made silver as common in Jerusalem as stones, and he made cedars as plentiful as fig trees in the foothills," (1 Ki. 10:27 GW)

Cyrus the Great

See Daniel 2, Nebuchadnezzar's dream of a huge image. According to Daniel's interpretation of the dream, Medo-Persia was to be the second most powerful kingdom in that known world after Babylon, represented by the chest and arms of silver in the dream. Medo-Persia overthrew the Babylonian empire through its king Cyrus. This Cyrus was prophesied 100 years before he was born and accurately called out by his name in the prophecy, see Isaiah 45:1-5.

Several versions of his birth and rise to power are recorded. Herodotus (i.95) mentions three. In that which he quotes (i.107ff), it is said that Mandane was the daughter of the Median king Astyages, who, in consequence of a dream which he had had, foretelling the ultimate triumph of her son over his dynasty, gave her in marriage to a Persian named Cambyses, who was not one of his peers. A second dream caused him to watch for her expected offspring, and when Cyrus came into the world Astyages delivered the child to his relative, Harpagus, with orders to destroy it. Being Unwilling to do this, he handed the infant to a Shepherd named Mitradates, who, his wife having brought forth a still-born child, consented to spare the life of the infant Cyrus.

Later on, in consequence of his imperious acts, Cyrus was recognized by Astyages, who came to learn the whole story, and spared him because, having once been made king by his companions in play, the Magians held the predictions concerning his ultimate royal state to have been fulfilled. The vengeance taken by Astyages upon Harpagus for his apparent disobedience to orders is well known: his son was slain, and a portion, disguised, given him to eat.

Though filled with grief, Harpagus concealed his feelings, and departed with the remains of his son's body; and Cyrus, in due course, was sent to stay with his parents, Cambyses and Mandane. Later on, Harpagus persuaded Cyrus to induce the Persians to revolt, and Astyages having blindly appointed Harpagus commander-in-chief of the Median army, the last-named went over to the side of Cyrus. The result was an easy victory for the latter, but Astyages took care to impale the Magians who had advised him to spare his grandson. Having gathered another, but a smaller, army, he took the field in person but was defeated and captured. Cyrus, however, who became king of Media as well as of Persia, treated him honorably and well.

John Bunyan

In 1655 when he was 27 years old he became a Baptist, for preaching to the Baptist congregation at Bedford he was thrown into prison, where he "tagged laces" twelve years and a half (1660-1672), and composed the Pilgrim's Progress, a work which has already gone through more than fifty editions, and has been translated into many foreign languages, this book has been the world's bestselling book only second to the Bible. Bunyan claimed to have received the narration of his book in a dream while imprisoned for preaching the gospel. The book has inspired and influenced men and women that went on to change the world. Abraham Lincoln read the book between the ages of 14 to 16. It's supposedly said that he read the whole of it over three to four times.

The dream before Jesus' crucifixion

Mat. 27:19 GW, *"While Pilate was judging the case* (Jesus' case), *his wife sent him a message. It said, "Leave that innocent man alone. I've been very upset today because of a dream I had about him."* She had a dream the night before Jesus' crucifixion that resulted in her warning her husband Pilate to have nothing to do with Jesus because He was an innocent man. This is no wonder why

Pilate washed his hands in front of the crowd and claimed he is innocent of the blood of this just man (Jesus), see Mat. 27:24.

Claudia Procula or Procla, Pilate's wife, the governor over Judaea which had been placed by the government of Rome. It necessitated that a governor should be a Roman citizen to be a governor. Jesus birth came at a time when Jews were colonized by Rome, tradition states that Claudia Procla was a proselyte of the gate, which is by no means unlikely, as many of the Jewish proselytes were women. By an imperial regulation provincial governors had been prohibited from taking their wives with them.

Chapter 9

DREAMS IN INVENTIONS

Madam C. J Walker (Entrepreneur)

The Guinness book of world records lists her as the first woman in history to start with nothing and ended up with a multimillion-dollar fortune in America, she made her fortune in the early 20th-century cosmetic industry, a black man had appeared to her in a dream and told her the mixture which would help her falling out hair grow back in. Beginning with two dollars and a dream by 1910 she set up her first shop in Indianapolis what she invented became a successful hair care formula and made her a magnate in the cosmetic industry.

Larry Page (Entrepreneur)

Google's co-founder, when he was 23 years old student, was searching for a Ph.D. topic and came up with the idea of super long ropes that could transport goods into earth's orbit he rejected the idea as being crazy and started turning to his dreams for inspiration. At a given night he dreamt of downloading the entire World Wide Web. It seemed as not the best idea. He woke up in the middle of his dream and thought of the idea of collecting the webpage instead. His writing began since he had found his Ph.D. proposal over time he realized he could rank those webpage links in a search by valuing sites that were linked to by a lot of other sites. This is how the Google search algorithm came into being. By the time of the writing of this book his net worth is $63.6 Billion at number 8 on the top 10 billionaires list and his business partner Sergey Brin coming up behind him at number 9.

Dr. James Watson

Dreamt two intertwined snakes with heads up at ends leading to his consideration of a double helix and so the structure of DNA was born.

James Cameron (Film creator)

One of my favorite film directors, writer, and producer, in his own words he says, *"A lot of stuff comes to me in dreams, I remember it sometimes it's an image and I'll go draw or paint that image."* In his interview statement, he claims the idea of Pandora, Avatar's magical land was from a dream in college having lived through book paintings waking up he quickly painted many of them as he could remember one of them was a glowing forest with a river of light running through it and trees that kind of looked like fiber optics 30 years later he made a movie that looks like that image that came to him in a dream when he was 18 years old (Avatar 2009). One time a fever spiking 39 degrees Celsius he had the idea of a terminator in a dream, Cameron saw the metallic figure with piercing red eyes pulling itself up out of the fire. Two of his most celebrated films are Titanic which was the 1997 all-time greatest grossing film worldwide and the second being Avatar which became the histories grossing film beating Titanic before its position was undone by the Avengers End Game.

Christopher Nolan (Film creator)

Also one of my top ten film directors, writer, and producer, mainly famous for directing, producing Inception, and is said to be fascinated with dreams he would frequently practice waking up and falling partially asleep again. This he would do to try manipulating his dreams in a semi-conscious state

Beethoven (Musician)

He is said to be a prolific dreamer he heard many of his piano sonatas in his dreams waking up he would write them down some historians claim in his dreams he would have featured instruments not yet invented.

Elias Howe and the sewing machine

He had the idea of a sewing machine with a needle that would go through a piece of cloth. But Howe seemed to could not figure out how it would work out. He dreamt cannibals trying to cook him while dancing around the fire with pointed spears. He noticed on the head of each spear was a tiny hole through the shaft. When he woke up, he could not shake his head off the up and down motion of the spears and their holes. The idea of passing the thread through the needle close to the point not on the other end became the backbone of the sewing machine.

Friedrich August Kekule and the discovery of benzene

It had been many years since scientists had been struggling to figure out the molecular structure of the benzene with little to no success to show for it. On a particular night, Friedrich had a dream of a group of snakes swallowing their tales by forming a seeming hexagon structure. After waking up the man cracked out the many years almost impossible structure of benzene. Before this in 1954 through dreams, he realized carbon likes to form straight lines during which the horses and carts became juggling atoms.

Albert Einstein and the theory of relativity

One-night Albert Einstein had a strange dream of cows approaching an electric fence where the farmer switched the fence on. He observed all the cows jumped back together when they got electrocuted. He discussed this with the farmer where he mentioned how the cows jumped back one by one. When he awoke, from the dream he got the idea that one observer may see things happen instantaneously while others may see the same event happen in a sequence. Thus, the governing principle of the theory of relativity was born.

Niels Bohr and the structure of the atom

Niels Bohr, Albert Einstein's friend and later known as the father of Quantum Mechanics discovered the structure of the atom through his dream. In the dream, he saw the nucleus of the atom with electronic spinning around it in similarity to how the planets spin around the sun. Immediately he returned to the lab upon searching he realized the evidence supports his dream. In this, the long and frustrating hours of trying to put together the final structure of the atom were gone.

Dmitri Mendeleev and the discovery of the periodic table

Dmitri undertook the daunting task of presenting all the discovered elements in a simple yet scientifically uncompromised way. After a strenuous time of arranging some elements in place for him to put all of them in place, the odds were against him. At a given night he had a dream of a table where all the elements fell into place as required. He wrote all that down into a piece of paper by 1869 what we now know as a periodic table was first published.

Jacob Dreams his way to wealth

Jacob received the blessing by usurping it since his father was blind. According to Jewish tradition, the blessing was supposed to be received by the elder son which was Esau his brother. Esau was indignant with Jacob. Jacob had to run for his life. He ran to Mesopotamia to his uncle Laban (Gen. 28-29).

Jacob's uncle Laban had two daughters, Leah the older and the younger Rachel. Rachel was beautiful and had a good-looking body. Jacob asked to work by tending the sheep of Laban for seven years, after seven years to be given Rachel. His uncle Laban agreed. After seven years, on the night of Jacob's wedding ceremony, his uncle had him drunk and he woke up the next morning having slept with Leah. Leah, the Bible never mentions her being beautiful except that she had beautiful eyes. I suppose she wasn't ideally appealing since Jacob never considered her. Being angry he confronted his uncle about the issue. Laban told Jacob that their tradition does not

Hearing God's voice in Dreams

allow the younger sister to get married ahead of the older one. He agreed to work for another seven years for Rachel. Laban gives him Rachel during the process (Gen. 29:18-28).

After fourteen years Jacob confronts Laban to release him. By this time Jacob had eleven sons born to him. Laban constrains him to stay and name the price he would desire of him. He had learned that God had blessed him because of Jacob, his flock had increased. Jacob agrees to work for him on one condition, that all the spotted, striped, and specked flock be his. This seemed impossible to Laban since all his flock that was left under Jacob's care was plain with no spots or stripes (Gen. 30:26-36).

During the season of the flock mating, Jacob cut the branches of the poplar, almond, and plane trees and then peeled the barks on them to reveal the white which was on the branches. He put these branches in the troughs, directly in front of the flock when they would come to drink. The flock mated in front of the branches and conceived. Whenever the weak would mate Jacob would pull out the troughs, he only did this to the strong. The flock produced striped, spotted and strong lambs, by so doing Jacob became very wealthy, had large flocks, camels, donkeys, female and male servants (Gen. 30:37-43).

His way of having flocks that were spotted and stripped has confounded great thinkers. It cannot be scientifically or rationally explained. In chapter 31:1 GW, *"Jacob heard that Laban's sons were saying, "Jacob has taken everything that belonged to our father and has gained all his wealth from him."* The Lord told Jacob to return to the land of his ancestors. From this point on Jacob called his wives in the field where he had been tending the flock and told them their father had changed toward him; he wasn't like before. Jacob explained to them a dream he had where he'd seen an Angel of the Lord, *"The angel of God spoke to me in the dream and said, 'Jacob!' 'Yes,' I answered. 'Look,' he continued, 'all the male goats that are mating are striped, spotted, and speckled. I am making this happen because I have seen all that Laban is doing to you,"* Gen. 31:11-12 GNB.

Our only explanation of Jacob's miracle to cause a plain flock to produce striped spotted and speckled lambs are the verse above. Before the flock's courtship season Jacob had a dream of the Angel of the Lord appearing to him and showing that He was going to cause the plain flock to produce striped, spotted, and speckled lambs. Jacob had this as a revelation through a dream. After this, he cut off branches and peeled the barks revealing the white part, and placed these peeled branches on the flock's troughs for when they came to drink. What Jacob was doing here was creating an environment conducive to the miracle. The last thing those sheep had seen during their mating was speckled and striped branches. This picture was programmed into the flock which is the latter the flock produced. Jacob received a spiritual complex revelation dream that produced him a strategy for wealth creation.

Joseph the Real Estate founder

Joseph is the eleventh son of Jacob, in fact, his favorite son. When at age 17 he had two dreams where he saw his father, mother, and eleven brothers bowing before him. His father loved him and brought him a coat of many colors. Joseph's eleven brothers hated him and sold him to the Ishmaelites. They took his coat of many colors and dipped it into an animal's blood to lie that he had been devoured by a wild animal. His father remained heart wrecked ever since.

The Ishmaelites took Joseph and sold him to Potiphar one of Pharaoh's officials and captain of guards. Joseph being a man of favor his master's wife forced him to sleep with her, the woman grabbed a hold of his cloak; he ran away leaving his cloak behind and she screamed. The workers attended to her and she lied that Joseph forced her to sleep with him. Potiphar threw Joseph into prison. In the prison, Joseph interpreted the dreams of Pharaoh's officials who were arrested. To the chief baker, the interpretation of

Hearing God's voice in Dreams

his dream was that after three days he would be executed and to the chief wine bearer, he told him Pharaoh was going to restore his position in the kingdom. Joseph urged the chief cup (wine) bearer to remember him after being restored. Both Pharaoh's officers were released out of prison and things happened to them according to Joseph's interpretations of their dreams but the chief cupbearer forgot Joseph (Gen. 39-40).

After two years Pharaoh had a dream standing on the banks of the river Nile. In the dream, he saw seven well-fed, nice looking cows coming out from the river and started grazing on the reeds. Seven other cows' skinny and sickly came out of the river from behind the seven well-fed cows and ate the seven well-fed cows. Pharaoh woke up and slept again. He dreamt another dream of seven healthy, good looking heads of grain growing from a single stalk and seven thin and scorched by the wind heads of grain sprouted from behind and swallowed the healthy, good looking heads of grain. He woke up from his sleep and was upset the whole morning.

Pharaoh summoned all his magicians, sorcerers, and the intellects of Egypt to interpret the dream to him. No one was able to interpret Pharaoh's dream. The chief cupbearer remembered Joseph and told Pharaoh about him, Pharaoh summoned and took Joseph out of prison. Joseph interpreted the dream to Pharaoh, *"Seven years are coming when there will be plenty of food in Egypt. After there will come seven years of famine, people will forget that there was plenty of food in Egypt, and the famine will ruin the land. People won't remember that there once was plenty of food in the land, because the coming famine will be so severe. The reason Pharaoh has had a recurring dream is because the matter has been definitely decided by God, and he will do it very soon,"* Gen. 41:29-32 GW added text.

"And Pharaoh said unto his servants, Can we find such a one as this is, a man in whom the Spirit of God is?" Gen. 41:38 ASV Emphasis added. Interestingly, Pharaoh being an Egyptian ruler

serving the gods of his people could perceive that there is a Spirit of God upon Joseph. Pharaoh placed Joseph over all Egypt after he said, *"There is no one as wise and intelligent as you,"* vs.39b GW. Pharaoh could pick it up that there is a Spirit of invention and creativity upon Joseph. This was the same Spirit that produced a strategy and tactic that has made any man or woman who followed it a billionaire to this age. *"You will be in charge of my palace, and all my people will do what you say. I will be more important than you, only because I'm Pharaoh." Then Pharaoh said to Joseph, "I now put you in charge of Egypt. Then Pharaoh took off his signet ring and put it on Joseph's finger. He had Joseph dressed in robes of fine linen and put a gold chain around his neck,"* Gen. 41:40-42 GW.

During the seven years of plenty, the Bible records that Joseph collected all the food grown in Egypt and stored it in cities. He stored up huge grain quantities like the sand in the seashore that he couldn't measure it anymore and gave up keeping any records. After the seven years of plenty had ended in Egypt the whole land experienced famine just as Joseph had predicted. The Egyptians went to Pharaoh who sent them to Joseph telling them to do whatever he commands them to do. When the people came to Joseph he opened up all the storehouses throughout the land and sold them the grain. All the countries came to Egypt to buy grain having experienced the famine as well (Gen. 41:48-57).

People came with large sums of money to buy from Joseph. Later people came to complain to Joseph that they have spent every bit of money they had and nothing was left of it now. He asked them what else they had in their possession. The people told him they had their livestock, he told them to bring it. The Egyptians exchanged their donkeys, goats, cattle, and horses for grain (Gen. 47:14-17). They went back to Joseph again, *"you know that our money is gone, and you have all our livestock. There's nothing left to bring you except our bodies and our land,"* Gen. 47:18b GW. This was the world's most devastating moment when Joseph would introduce a strategy and a tactic that would be the world's vehicle for more efficient and steady wealth creation. People were indignantly complaining on the while, *"Take us and our land in exchange for food. Then we will be Pharaoh's slaves and our land will be his property. But give us seed so that we won't starve to death and the ground won't become a desert,"* Gen. 47:19 GW.

Joseph having the Spirit of God upon him, the Spirit Which Pharaoh perceived, the Spirit of creativity, the Father of every great invention brought a master solution idea, *"Joseph bought all the land in Egypt for Pharaoh. Every Egyptian sold his fields because the famine was so severe. The land became Pharaohs. Joseph said to the people, "Now that I have bought you and your land for Pharaoh, here is seed for you. Plant crops in the land. Every time you harvest, give one-fifth of the produce to Pharaoh. Four-fifths will be yours to use as seed for your fields and as food for your households,* "Gen.47:20, 23-24 GW. Here is an idea that has also shaped and changed centuries over five thousand years ago, brought for the first time by Joseph, a man that had the Spirit of God upon him, the interpreter of dreams, a man with a Michah Mantle as mentioned in the first chapter of this book.

Pharaoh's dreams gave him a word of wisdom concerning the future. This is known today as Real Estate, French 'Royal Estate.' The idea has traveled further through the centuries to even Europe where the Royal families have used it for their selfish gains to oppress the poor, by then known as the Feudal system. It has been the vehicle today that has made most of the world's billionaires, namely, Donald Trump of the Trump Estates, Ray Kroc of the McDonalds, Erin Carlyle, Lee ShauKee, Donald Bren, Stephen Ross, Leonard Stern, etc. Many years ago, a study concluded that 90% of millionaires in the U.S made it from Real Estate. There are 256 billionaires in the world doing Real Estate in 2020 according to *Forbes*.

Chapter 10

HOW TO STOP BAD DREAM PREDICTIONS

Dreams can fall under the category of prophecy especially when they are predicting an aspect of the future instead of just being a warning or a message of exhortation to you. Dreams that fall under prophecy fall under two categories, conditional prophecy dreams, and the unconditional prophecy dream.

Conditional prophecy dreams are dreams whose predicted future you can change and unconditional prophecy dreams are dreams whose future you cannot change. To know the difference requires you to know the revealed will of God through His Word. There are three wills of God according to Romans 12:2, the goodwill of God, the permissive or call it the acceptable will of God, and the perfect will of God. Most of the Lord's children are living under the permissive will of God.

To reach the perfect will of God we have to have our minds constantly transformed because the flesh daily wars against the will of God and religion has taught us that God wants us to suffer to keep us holy, that when we sick, broke, and poor is either God is training or teaching us a lesson. We have to discern the difference here to know what type of dream course needs to be altered. Suffering with Christ does not mean consenting to poverty, sickness, and demonic oppression. There is a teaching that has gone out to say God trains a believer even through sickness. God is not confused to deliver us from sickness and then train us with the sickness; this doctrine nullifies the work of the cross. If God will use such, what His Son has died for is in vain and it seems fit to say He initiated the fall of men which is not biblical.

According to the Bible, ALL sickness is from the devil, not God, Act 10:38 GW, *"How God anointed Jesus of Nazareth with the*

Holy Ghost and with power: who went about doing good and healing all that were oppressed of the devil; for God was with him." All the people that Jesus healed or delivered were oppressed by the devil, not God.

Christ has delivered us from everything that pertains to the fall; the only thing He hasn't delivered us from is from people. This is to say men can persecute us for the Gospel as much as they possibly can, this is the suffering the Bible permits us to go through:

> *Jesus answering said, Verily I say to you, There is no one who has left house, or brethren, or sisters, or father, or mother, or wife, or children, or lands, for my sake and for the sake of the gospel, that shall not receive a hundredfold now in this time: houses, and brethren, and sisters, and mothers, and children, and lands, with persecutions, and in the coming age life eternal.* Mar 10:29-30 Darby.

We are promised a hundredfold in this life in relationships, property, and possessions but with persecution. To read more on this topic see my blog post why was Jesus standing from His throne when Stephen was stoned on www.nicholasvmbanjwa.com. So when you happen to dream a dream and it predicts poverty or sickness for either you or any of your loved ones upon waking up immediately cast it out it is not part of your Salvation package.

When you are asleep your body, the flesh is quiet your spirit is more alive notice in the immediate hours of waking up that you can vividly recall your dreams. During that time of your waking up, your spirit will normally tell you what is wrong about the dream, you might sense an alert or awaiting danger as revealed by the dream or possibly a weird environment around you. In this case, you need to pray in the spirit. Praying in the spirit is praying in an unknown tongue (see Acts 2:4). It is every believer's right to pray in the spirit. If you don't know how to pray in the spirit arrange to talk to any church leader you have heard pray in an unknown tongue and ask them to help you receive this precious gift. I will also give a summary at the end of this book to help you receive this gift as you don't necessarily need a pastor.

> *At the same time, the Spirit also helps us in our weakness, because we don't know how to pray for what we need. But the Spirit intercedes along with our groans that cannot be expressed in words. The one who searches our hearts knows what the Spirit has in mind. The Spirit intercedes for God's people the way God wants him to. We know that all things work together for the good of those who love God- those whom he has called according to his plan.* Rom. 8:26-28 GW.

In the words of the above verse we know not what we should pray for as we ought, the Spirit, capital letter S for the Holy Spirit intercedes for us through groans that cannot be expressed in words. When praying in the spirit (your spirit), you ignite the Holy Spirit capital letter S inside your spirit and He prays through your spirit such that you may end up feeling torrents of rivers flowing inside of you or rather a fountain welling up on the inside of you this then develops to groans where at times you run out of words and tears stream down your cheeks in your secret place. He is praying for you in your shortcomings that word is the Greek word astheneia which can also be translated as weakness of mind or emotional weakness.

The Holy Spirit is outside of time He sees both the past and future simultaneously when He prays through you He prays ahead in time. Just keep your mind stayed on that alert you sense in your spirit that you had picked up since waking up from your dream. Stay your mind on it because your mind is a powerful tool in the realm of the spirit that is why the devil uses it against God and to condemn you. God also yearns to use that mind too. Eph. 3:20 GW, *"Now to him that is able to do exceeding abundantly above all that we ask or think* (the power of your mind), *according to the power that worketh in us."* The power of our mind releases the resurrection power stored up on the inside of us. So when praying in tongues the Holy Spirit releases this resurrection power to the area of your focused need, where your mind is stayed.

Don't let unnecessary thoughts distract your mind during this time of prayer from being stayed on what you want to be changed. Focus your mind on it as you pray until you sense a tone of victory in your spirit where you once sensed awaiting danger. By this, you will know you have changed the course of your destiny or your loved ones' destiny. Sometimes this alert of awaiting danger may linger for an hour and you may be willing to give up in 15 minutes as you will sense no change but remember the heroes of old, *"that ye be not sluggish, but imitators of them who through faith and patience inherit the promises."* Heb. 6:12 ASV.

We have been taught so much in the area of faith but have never been taught to apply the virtue of patience to our faith. It is here where we know no failure. Whether we pray for two hours nonstop in the spirit we have the assurance that He (God the Father) that searches our hearts (spirits of man) knows what is the mind of the Spirit (God the Holy Spirit's will and intents) as we pray in Christ Jesus (God the Son) it is here where we know, or convicted that all things work together for the good of those who love the Lord, the called according to His purpose. Cultivating a life of consistent prayer in the spirit is another way to developing your spirit for dominion and constant victory. *"The one speaking in a tongue builds* (edifies) *himself up."* 1 Cor. 14:4 LITV. *"But you, my beloved, building yourselves upon your most holy faith, praying in the Holy Ghost..."* Jud. 20 DRB.

Sometimes the Lord is graceful enough that the Holy Spirit makes you pray in the dream and you find yourself praying even when you wake up from it. Here also the Lord is altering the course of your destiny through you. It was Wesley who once remarked, *"It seems God cannot do anything unless we pray."* Do know that the type of dream you just dreamt was spiritual warfare but the Lord dealt with whatever lingering attack from the enemy was set against you in that very dream.

Unconditional prophecy dream, based on your knowledge of your purpose, calling, and will of God for your life you are able to discern unconditional prophecy dreams to make this sound less complicated let's just say it is based on your knowledge of the will of God for your life as revealed in His written Word.

Years ago before I met my wife I was in a serious dating process with a particular lady. This was some years since I had finished high school. I had grown in years and spiritually therefore I was ready to date. Everything was going well and I was planning we take the relationship to new heights until I began having a premonition that I was not going to end up with the girl in the future. I knew it was God speaking to me through my spirit. I began investing myself into hours of prayer seeking a deeper understanding from God. In the course of the prayer while in the relationship I had three notable dreams.

In one particular dream, I was inside a structure filled with Saints it seemed like a prayer gathering. In the dream, I knew the girl was also present in that gathering but each time I tried to look around for her I couldn't find nor see her. This was a wide-open structure with people not more than 70 I was supposed to easily see her in the crowd. On waking up I struggled to understand the dream. The other two dreams were the same context and the same outcome even though the contents differed. It was after all three dreams were I finally understood that the dreams are showing me we won't end up together with the young lady that I finally began to pray to change the prediction. In my mind, I thought it was because the devil would stand in the way. I don't think I told her the dreams since once I tried to tell her about what I was sensing she thought I was being negative.

Hearing God's voice in Dreams

Time lapsed things changed in the relationship we no longer had peace, the more we tried to work things out the more we grew apart until after a time of fighting to pull things together we finally let loose of the relationship. After a year or two when the relationship had ended, it was then that I began to know the devil had nothing to do with it, it was God. God saw our incompatibility and allowed the relationship not to work out no matter how much I prayed that the relationship work out no amount of prayer could change God's mind. One of my deeply held values was to stay in one relationship for the rest of my life without moving from one relationship to another.

The above is an example of unconditional prophecy dream because it concerned the will of God concerning who I was supposed to marry, like unconditional prophecies we cannot change the predicted outcomes of such dreams. After all, we would foolishly imply to be changing God's established will concerning our lives. In such instances, we can only pray that the participants involved be not severely hurt by their choices but healed or preserved during or after the outcomes.

Chapter 11

HOW TO HAVE MORE DREAMS AND REMEMBER THEM

We oftentimes struggle to remember our dreams. Most people who remember their dreams are the ones who wake up between 5 am and 7 am. These seem to be refreshing hours for the mind. Below in their respective order are some of the best ways to start seeing more dreams and remembering them.

The first important key to getting more dreams and remembering them is to exercise yourself in spiritual consciousness by this I am not advocating for spiritual science. Since we are spirit, soul, and body as believers it is important to develop ourselves spiritually and God desires that we grow spiritually. I am convinced that some of our national challenges be it in business, community, or family would be mitigated by Christians if we understood this one aspect. Adam the first man was dominated by his spirit before the fall it was after the fall that his senses took over.

Therefore, Adam was more conscious of the spiritual world than the physical, the realm of the spirit was more real to him than his very heartbeat. Gen. 3:7 KJV, *"And the eyes of them both were opened, and they knew that they were naked; and they sewed fig leaves together, and made themselves aprons."* The Hebrew word for knew in this verse is *yada* which implies that Adam and Eve became sensual and the word also means feel which proves again that they began to be led by their senses. Adam before that was led by wisdom, the divine wisdom not the devilish one. His spirit man inside the body led his soul (mind, will, and emotions) and his soul led his body (senses). Not forgetting that the spirit man is the real you inside the body. God challenging Job's wisdom makes mention of the first man's wisdom, which wisdom sprung from his (Adam's) spirit that was created in the image and likeness of God, Job 15:7-8 GW, *"Were you the first human to be born? Were you delivered before the hills existed? Did you listen in on God's council meeting and receive a monopoly on wisdom?"*

The Bible states that as God's man all the animals and everything that creeps on the ground was presented to him to name (Gen. 2:19). Now if we would only count the bacterium apart from the animals they amount to about five hundred thousand that is almost half of a million. Mind you, Adam didn't have a notebook and a pen to record their names. He was purely operating in his perfect state.

After the fall Adam relied on his senses, he had to touch a stone and feel it to know it was rough. From our forefather Adam we have been operating from the outside in, we have been receiving knowledge from our senses no longer ruled by the spirit. If you do recall you will remember that in the 5th chapter we dealt with the different types of dreams. Which is godly and demonic dreams. Under godly dreams, we have three and under demonic dreams, we have two types.

All in all, we have five spiritual dreams and only one that is natural, the category being the Soulish Dreams. In layman's words, five types of dreams are from the spirit and only one type is from your soul. So to get you to be sharp in perceiving your important dreams, spiritual dreams we have to get you to know how to develop your spiritual senses as this will help you in remembering your dreams and by increasing your ability to dreaming more, not only to dream more but to also be very intuitively sharp.

The Bible in mentioning man's three faculties always begins with the spirit and ends with the body. 1Th. 5:23 KJV, *"And the very God of peace sanctify you wholly; and I pray God your whole spirit and soul and body be preserved blameless unto the coming of our Lord Jesus Christ."* Often when we make mention of these faculties we ignorantly say body, spirit, and soul. We start from the outside in. This not only exposes our ignorance but it also reveals our consciousness of the flesh (senses) first and then the spirit after. The Holy Spirit through the apostle Paul shows us the rightful order and is also insinuating that we are conscious of the spirit man first, then the soul, and lastly the body.

How to be conscious of the things of the spirit

We are spiritual beings living in a physical world that is dictated by the spirl world. Almost all human activity is derived or control in the spiritual realm you will remember the study we previously dealt with on the title of angels and how the diabolic angels influence the affairs of human life on a daily to daily basis. We know that according to the Bible Satan is the god of this world, world as in system (see 2 Cor. 4:4, Joh. 12:31).

The devil usurped Adam's dominion. He will continue until Christ's second coming (see Mat 8:28-29). That is the reason why we have a different system in God's kingdom. Who crucified Jesus? It wasn't the Jews nor the Romans, *"But we speak the wisdom of God in a mystery, even the hidden wisdom, which God ordained before the world unto our glory: Which none of the princes of this world knew: for had they known it, they would not have crucified the Lord of glory."* 1 Cor. 2:7-8 KJV. The princes of this world mentioned in the preceding verse are not the earthly government of the time but the diabolic spirits in the spiritual world (see Eph. 6:12).

Many of the evil constitutionalized ideas in the current judicial system have their root from here. To mention a few, abortion, legalized same-sex marriages the list goes on. In short, life is spiritual. If God would open our eyes for us to see in the realms of the spirit we would lose our minds. There are vicious violent wars every day, angels of good battling the angels of darkness. It is a war against and for our lives. We have to be conscious of the spiritual world because to lay claim of our daily victories we have to control them from the spiritual world.

Hearing God's voice in Dreams

To live in victory we have to control the affairs of our lives from the realm of the spirit. To be conscious of the things of the spirit we have to learn to exercise God's presence. God's presence is unleashed in obedience. Every single day God speaks to us, every single day the Holy Spirit leads us. We have to start small to believe God to guide us in the big decisions of our lives. The Kingdom principle for multiplication is that if we can be faithful with little God will entrust us with much. The Lord constantly speaks to us through our spirits, intuition, conscience, and instincts. He will sometimes tell us what to give, where to give, who to listen to in the areas of the gospel, where to fellowship, and how to serve in ministries He has planted us.

As a married man, I would sometimes say something to my wife and feel my conscience unsettled until I apologize to her. There be many ways the Lord leads us from day today. The more we listen and obey Him the more we become conscious of the things of the spirit. At times we want to make major decisions as to who to marry, which career path to take, should you partner with that person in business or not. We are not supposed to act out emotionally or mentally. We are to be led by God, the just shall live by faith (see Heb. 10:38). Before we make such major decisions if we have no clarity in our spirits we dare separate ourselves for at least 3 days, whether in prayer or fasting and meditation of the Word until we receive a direction in our spirits.

Don't seek out an audible voice for you will open yourself prey to demons. Look out for that green or red alert in your spirit. If you happen to sense a green alert in your spirit you are to go on with the decision. Should you sense a red alert, unsettled, or empty in your spirit discard the decision because God is warning you against such. Many times we struggle following the leading in our spirits because we perceive through our sight that the decision has got to be it as Lot chose the beautiful, green watered land before him while Abraham set out to the parched lands. Abraham was a man of faith, he understood it is the Lord that brings springs from the desert lands.

Hearing God's voice in Dreams

Lot in following his sense of sight set out to a land which would later be famous for its lasciviousness, Sodom. In setting a time to pray and seek the Lord concerning major decisions of our lives we will ultimately be more sensitive to the spirit that we will no longer need to set aside time in the future but will instantly know the Lord's leading when just thinking about it. We learn to be sensitive and more conscious of the things of the spirit. This also helps to increase our capacity to dream more dreams. Some individuals dream an average of 3 to 5 dreams per night.

How to deal with blurry dreams

If your dreams are blurry or you often dream of being haunted by your past or a certain sin you might have done in the past keeps on coming in dreams. The problem is due to condemnation that is undealt with. Condemnation can affect how your dreams turn out or how you as a participant in a dream perceive things. As a child of God, your only way of dealing with condemnation is to study the work of the blood from the Scriptures. Heb. 9:14 KJV, *"How much more shall the blood of Christ, who through the eternal Spirit offered himself without spot to God, purge your conscience from dead works to serve the living God?"*

It is only through the revelation of the blood of Jesus that sin condemnation can be cured. To deal with condemnation sum up all the New Testament Scriptures that deal with the blood and write them down on a piece of paper and personalize them, here is an example using the above verse, *"How much more shall the blood of Christ, who through the eternal Spirit offered himself without spot to God, purge (My) conscience from dead works to serve the living God?"*. After you have personalized each verse you have collected confess them every morning until they become your consciousness. When you dream being chased or fighting that is a spiritual warfare dream or any dream where you running away from an animal you are prone to come across such dreams once in a while but when you always have such types of dreams you might have to introspect yourself whether you are not demonic conscious than God-conscious. A lot of Christians are demon conscious because of bombarding themselves with demon-centric messages which cause them to often be oppressed during sleeping hours or through dreams.

You can also partake of the Lord's Supper alone as much as you want:

> *Then after he had given thanks, he broke it and said, "This is my body, which is given for you. Eat this and remember me." After the meal, Jesus took a cup of wine in his hands and said, "This is my blood, and with it God makes his new agreement with you. Drink this and remember me." The Lord meant that when you eat this bread and drink from this cup, you tell about his death until he comes.* (1 Cor. 11:24-26 GW).

Notice the King James Version on verse 26, *"For as often as ye eat this bread, and drink this cup, ye do shew the Lord's death till he come."* The word shew is the same Greek word used in Acts 4:2, 13:5, 38, 15:36, in all these instances it is translated preached. Meaning whenever we partake of the Lord's Supper we preach to God because the blood was meant for God, Jesus offered the blood to God, not to the devil and we preach to sicknesses, diseases, sin, and death for it was the body of Jesus that took our sins, curses, pains, and afflictions upon itself. When we partake we declare the Lord's victory over all infirmities and in the face of defeat.

Also notice the opening word, "often," in Greek the word means many times as. There is no limit stipulated, often can be as many as 3 times a day in the next coming three days or for the whole week. Google Smith Wigglesworth, he had a stunning record of raising 22 people from the dead. His message was solely on faith and it's recorded that every morning he partook of the Lord's Supper. Faith in the revelation of the blood is as bold as a lion and a great cure for condemnation.

Chapter 12

HOW TO INTERPRET DREAMS Pt 1

In this chapter, we will look at why the Lord uses symbols in dreams and how dreams were interpreted in Bible times. In the following chapter, we will look at how we can use the same method to interpret dreams today and I will demonstrate using some peoples' dreams, dreams I have interpreted before. Do not concern yourself with the items in dreams for now we will deal with them in the second part of this book.

The greatest thing I learned about God through His Word is that He is very intentional and very detailed as a result every detail in Scripture is by deliberate design. The colors, the numbers, even the measurements of the Tabernacle and its vessels, the description of certain garments are all placed there perfectly by the hand of the Holy Spirit without a single contradiction. If you think because you different God will communicate to you using the same colors but in a different meaning that is to deceive yourself, a righteous and truthful God has to maintain His integrity and not change His language. The Holy Spirit who brings us dreams is the same Person we all as believers have, so we maintain that the method of communication and means conveyed will always remain uniform, Heb 13:8 Weymouth, *"Jesus Christ is the same yesterday and to-day--yes, and to the ages to come."* And for Him to change His means and methods of communication will be to elucidate that He is not eternal (outside of time). Change can only come with time.

Why are dreams symbolic?

Rom. 1:20 GW, *"From the creation of the world, God's invisible qualities, his eternal power, and divine nature, have been observed in what he made. As a result, people have no excuse."* Spiritual things cannot be fathomed by any man, no man can know

Hearing God's voice in Dreams

the things that be of God except the spirit of God in him or her. For God to communicate to men successfully His terms and the concepts He uses to communicate with us must be common and relevant to our day to day language and experiences so that He can be relevant and relative, in that way we can understand the message conveyed or passed down to us. If He were to speak to us as He is it would have been harder for any of us to understand. His wisdom is vastly greater than anything we can comprehend.

Men's wisdom is a drop in the ocean when compared to God's. Thus, when God came in the flesh He spoke to His audience in parables. Parables help to conceal a message in case the recipient is not ready so that when the recipient is matured, in the right and proper time he or she may fathom the message. Mat. 13:10-11 GW, *"The disciples asked him, "Why do you use stories as illustrations when you speak to people?" Jesus answered, "Knowledge about the mysteries of the kingdom of heaven has been given to you. But it has not been given to the crowd."* The newest member in the Kingdom of God has access to the knowledge of mysteries of the Kingdom of heaven. Here are a few examples of topics covered by Jesus on parables concerning the Kingdom:

- A parable on building (Mat. 7:24-27)
- A parable on winemaking (Lk. 5:37-38)
- A parable on seed (Mar. 4:2-20)
- A parable on treasure hunting (Matt. 13:44)
- A parable on ranching (Mat. 13:44)
- A parable on laborers in the vineyard (Matt. 20:1-16)
- Parable of two sons (Matt. 21:28-31)
- A parable on hostile takeover (Lk. 20:9-19)
- A parable on talents (Mat. 25:14-30)

- A parable on Future market (Lk. 12:16-21)
- A parable on weeds (Mar. 13:27-32)
- A parable on management criteria (Lk. 12:35-48)
- The need for observation and research (Lk. 14:24-35)
- Parable of the prodigal son (Lk. 15:11-16)
- Parable of the dishonest manager (Lk. 16:1-13)

In the above parables, we have a heavenly language conveyed in human's daily experiences to get spiritual things unveiled. The book of Revelation is a very great example of this, Sir W.M Ramsey researched the seven churches of Revelation archaeologically. Laodicea stood midway between the hot springs of river Hierapolis and the cold river of Colossae, the city was fed by an aqueduct from Hierapolis that carried both hot and cold water. When it arrived in the city it was lukewarm. Rev. 3:16 GW, *"But since you are lukewarm and not hot or cold, I'm going to spit you out of my mouth."* I have found this allegorical approach used by Jesus to be exceptionally interesting. The Lord speaks to the Laodicea church using an allegory they would be acquainted with. Like in dreams and visions the Lord uses elements we are well affiliated with.

Psychological way of dream interpretation

As once mentioned in this detailed study we will only focus on the biblical way of interpreting dreams. Js. 3:15-17 KJV, *"This wisdom descendeth not from above, but is earthly, sensual, devilish. For where envying and strife is, there is confusion and every evil work. But the wisdom that is from above is first pure, then peaceable, gentle, and easy to be intreated, full of mercy and good fruits, without partiality, and hypocrisy."* The preceding verse teaches us the two kinds of wisdom, one from above (God) and one from the devil which is also natural, coming from the nature of the fallen man. The interpretation of dreams using psychology is a natural wisdom, the fallen man's wisdom. This type of wisdom fails to apprehend the spiritual realities that man is spirit and has spiritual problems, that his sicknesses, diseases, sin, and death are spiritual. It minimizes man to merely a soul and a body. It is independent of God.

Psychology never solves any problems but only deduce man to his actions, it tries to eliminate man's guilt and condemnation but will never eradicate his/her root problem, sin. People that resort to interpreting dreams using psychological methods end up leaving the dreamers mostly depressed, feeling empty, and open people's spirits to spiritual oppression. This is devilish wisdom.

The African way of dream interpretation

The African fundamental belief system is ancestry worship. Under normal circumstances, we have born again leaders and believers still affected by the traditional beliefs that have long altered their perceptions on spiritual issues. This is easily perceptible in the African idolatry paradigm that people have crossed with from the ancestry worship to the church of God unchanged, an example is the man of God dependence. We have photos in our homes presumed to protect the followers and even the excessive use of the anointing oil that we have easily slid away from the immutable power of the name of Jesus that when the oil is finished believers under attack feel powerless despite the ever-present name of Jesus.

Even when it comes to dreams interpretation the same rules apply. The ancestry worship has an aversion to civilization, sometimes having to imply that any technological advancement might carry a trail of fear with it due to these three reasons:

1. The belief that there is something spiritual about poverty, take a look at spiritual doctors.

2. Nothing happens in life except what is predetermined, causing some to hold that their fate in life is to be poor.
3. The spirit of poverty, when I say spirit in this context I refer to the perception and attitude, not a demon. A poverty mentality creates an apologetic spirit (attitude), someone trapped by such mentality is sorry for acquiring anything worthwhile because of the guilt inflicted by their beliefs. When they own anything good or things are seemingly going well they expect calamity because of the above reasons they feel they owe the ones who have not (I am not against giving but biblical giving is not based on feeling you owe your success to others rather it is based on love).

Say one dream of being in an airplane and seeks for an interpretation from any one of the ancestry worshippers, due to the native Africans filters of fear there always will follow a negative stimulus toward such a dream as stipulated by the three reasons given above. The first reaction is what could go wrong with an airplane. Therefore, the interpretation will be of interpreting the dream to mean death or one's coffin. If you are an African you know exactly what I mean (A biblical interpretation will never bring fear, condemnation, confusion, unbelief, and discouragement).

In common sense, no one boards a plane for their death. We board a plane to travel from one destination to another either due to distance or to save time. An airplane flies on-air, common sense calls for us to interpret this to mean a ministry (a mode of transport that takes people and goods from one place to another). On-air means something that operates above the land this means a higher spiritual calling or international traveling ministry (Biblical dream interpretation will bring correction, reproof, exhortation, comfort, and edification).

Hearing God's voice in Dreams

Here's a second example, say someone dreams of picking up plump and good pears from the ground. Native Africans are always prone to interpret such dreams to mean sickness, being initiated to something evil, bad luck, or misfortune. Somewhere in this chapter, we used the following analogy on dreams based on Revelation 3:16 GW, *"But since you are lukewarm and not hot or cold, I'm going to spit you out of my mouth."* Sir W.M Ramsey researched the seven churches of Revelation archaeologically.

Laodicea stood midway between the hot springs of river Hierapolis and the cold river of Colossae, the city was fed by an aqueduct from Hierapolis that carried both hot and cold water. When it arrived in the city of Laodicea it was lukewarm. Hence, *"You are neither cold nor hot... you are lukewarm"*, I have found this allegorical approach used by Jesus to be exceptionally interesting. The Lord speaks to this church using an allegory they would be acquainted with.

Like in dreams and visions the Lord uses elements we are well affiliated with. In the example of a plump and good pear it means exactly what we are affiliated with, pears are in the season of harvest, a plump and good pear means what is ripe and rich to be harvested. A pear is for eating. This, in common sense, means nothing but blessings if not fruitfulness (sometimes a fruit of the womb to a woman), a pleasant experience coming to your life, or abundance.

Learning from Joseph

We are going to glimpse into Joseph's way of interpreting dreams to learn the biblical way of dream interpretation. People who are filled with the Word of God hardly encounter a hard time interpreting dreams. The Bible has a great explanation of symbols.

> *And Joseph dreamt a dream, and he told it his brethren: and they hated him yet the more. And he*

said unto them, Hear, I pray you, this dream which I have dreamt: For, behold, we were binding sheaves in the field, and, lo, my sheaf arose, and also stood upright; and, behold, your sheaves stood round about, and made obeisance to my sheaf." Genesis 37:5-7 KJV

This is Joseph's first recorded dream. Let us look at how his brother's interpreted it. This is one of the easiest dreams in the Bible to be interpreted. The first and important rule is understanding that our dreams are not so much literal but are mostly allegorical. According to the English Dictionary, an allegory is a symbolic representation that can be interpreted to reveal a hidden meaning. We will look at them:

1. *Context:* This is what the whole dream is about. In this case, the dream is about harvest and Joseph. In the Jewish context, the field represents the world.

2. *Items:* items are the objects surrounding the dream. Here we are dealing with sheaves which represent the time or season of harvest.

3. *Persona* (Character(s)): This can be an animal or an individual seen in the dream. Sometimes these people or animals in dreams represent a hidden meaning. In this case, Joseph saw himself and his eleven brothers. Here the dream pointed to them. They were not representing anything hidden, but rather were all the subject of the dream.

NB: the best way to tell whether an item or a persona (character) in a dream is an allegory is when the item or persona has a feature that is out of the natural laws, an example is a purple cow or a single note of 1000 U.S dollars or South African rands. Naturally, we do not have a purple cow or a single money note that is 1000 American dollars or South African rands.

Hearing God's voice in Dreams

Context: Joseph dreamt of binding sheaves with his eleven brothers in the field and his sheaf arose and stood upright. Their sheaves stood all around and bowed down to Joseph's sheaf.

Items: The elements present in Joseph's dream. His sheaf standing upright represents the excellence of personal work bringing Joseph to influence and a position. His brother's sheaves bowing down to Joseph's sheaf, sheaves were the food of the time which can also represent famine and his brother's finding solution and maintenance through Joseph's position and influence.

By breaking down this dream we already see the whole destiny of Joseph laid before our very own eyes. The following is a section we did touch in chapter 9 concerning dreams in inventions when we looked at Joseph's idea that came to be known as real estate, though we will touch a part of that section in the context of how Joseph's first recorded dream revealed his whole destiny. Joseph dreamt the dream at age 17 he had his eleven brothers hating him and sold him to the Ishmaelites.

The Ishmaelites took Joseph and sold him to Potiphar one of Pharaoh's officials and captain of guards. Joseph being a man of favor his master's wife forced him to sleep with her, the woman grabbed a hold of his cloak; he ran away leaving his cloak behind and she screamed. The workers attended to her and she lied that Joseph forced her to sleep with him. Potiphar threw Joseph into prison. We know how in prison Joseph interpreted the dreams of Pharaoh's officials who were arrested.

To the chief baker, the interpretation of his dream was that after three days he would be executed and to the chief wine bearer, he told him Pharaoh was going to restore his position in the kingdom. Joseph urged the chief cup (wine) bearer to remember him after being restored (below we will look into the chief cupbearer and chief baker's dream interpretation in detail). Both Pharaoh's officers were released out of prison and things happened to them according to Joseph's interpretations of their dreams but the chief cupbearer forgot Joseph (Gen. 39-40). We will also look into both these dreams in this very chapter.

After two years Pharaoh had two dreams. Pharaoh summoned all his magicians, sorcerers, and the intellects of Egypt to interpret the dream to him. No one was able to interpret Pharaoh's dream. The chief cupbearer remembered Joseph and told Pharaoh about him, they hastily took him out of prison. Joseph interpreted the dreams of Pharaoh. *"And Pharaoh said unto his servants, Can we find such a one as this is, a man in whom the Spirit of God is?"* Gen. 41:38 GW. Interestingly, Pharaoh placed Joseph over all Egypt after he said, *"There is no one as wise and intelligent as you,"* vs.39b. *"You will be in charge of my palace, and all my people will do what you say. I will be more important than you, only because I'm Pharaoh."* Then Pharaoh said to Joseph, *"I now put you in charge of Egypt. Then Pharaoh took off his signet ring and put it on Joseph's finger. He had Joseph dressed in robes of fine linen and put a gold chain around his neck,"* Gen. 41:40-42 GW.

Let us recall his dream, *"For, behold, we were binding sheaves in the field, and, lo, my sheaf arose, and also stood upright; and, behold, your sheaves stood round about, and made obeisance to my sheaf."* Gen. 37:7 KJV. When the famine was severe in the land Joseph's brothers left Canaan to Egypt (the world, the field according to Joseph's dream) to buy corn sent by their father. Joseph sent them back to collect their eleventh brother Benjamin before he released them grain they did not recognize him. When they came with Benjamin it was on the second visit that Joseph conspired against them when he secretly put a royal cup in Benjamin's sack tricking them. Upon them leaving the city Joseph's steward followed and overtook them charging them with stealing his lord's cup by such means they were required to return to Egypt. After all the scheming he finally revealed his identity to them. *"And they bowed down their heads, and made obeisance."* Gen. 43:28b KJV.

Joseph interprets the chief butler's dream

Hearing God's voice in Dreams

N.B before we deal with the dreams Joseph interpreted learn that every dream you dream will either fall under a positive or a negative context. Note, the chief butler's dream has a positive context as the chief baker's dream carries a negative context. Distinguishing this will help you know whether the symbols in the dream carry a positive or negative meaning as you will learn later every element in dreams has both a negative and positive meaning. Example: let's use a lion, let's say you dream of walking with a lion.

That is a positive context dream which being interpreted symbolizes your walk with the Lord Jesus, the King of kings, in the Scriptures, He is called the Lion of the tribe of Judah (see Rev 5:5). For a negative dream, context let's say you dream of a lion chasing you. In this analogy, the lion symbolizes the devil in the Scriptures the devil is stated as roaring like a lion seeking whom he may devour (see 1 Pet. 5:8).

Joseph in prison encountered a scenario where two of his inmates were perplexed by dreams they dreamt the same night. Both these men were Pharaoh's officials. According to the first verse of Genesis 40, both these officials had offended their master which resulted in them being imprisoned. The first dream was that of the chief cupbearer:

> *So the chief cupbearer told Joseph his dream. He said "In my dream, a grapevine with three branches appeared in front of me. Soon after it sprouted it blossomed. Then its clusters ripened into grapes. Pharaoh's cup was in my hand, so I took the grapes and squeezed them into it. I put the cup in Pharaoh's hand." (Gen. 40:9-11 KJV).*

You will notice a pearl of supernatural wisdom as we look at how Joseph interpreted this particular dream. *"Do not interpretations belong to God?"* Gen. 40:8 KJV, notice the question Joseph imposed on the dreamers before he gave them the interpretation. The question reveals he consciously knew God as the source of dream

Hearing God's voice in Dreams

interpretation. This supernatural wisdom is not for the elite but all the children of God, *"He (Christ) was made unto us wisdom from God."* 1 Cor. 1:30 GW. The question is how do you access this wisdom? Today we access it through His Word, like looking to symbols used in the Bible to find meaning to our dreams. Sometimes we might not find the Bible's vivid meaning on the symbol of our dreams then here we have to access this wisdom by faith.

Joseph told the dreamers to tell him their dreams, notice, he needed to hear the dreams before he could interpret them meaning he had no interpretation until he heard the dream. This requires belief in God to come through. The chief cupbearer dreamt a grapevine with three branches appearing in front of him and they soon sprouted and blossomed then its clusters ripened into grapes. Pharaoh's cup was in his hand as he took the grapes and squeezed them into it. He then submitted the cup to Pharaoh. Below we will follow the C.I.P concept:

- Context: the dream is about the grapevine and the cupbearer. It carries a positive context as the cupbearer serves Pharaoh Wine as he always did before being imprisoned.
- Items: the grapevine, branches, and clusters.
- Persona: Pharaoh and the cupbearer.

Joseph interpreted the three branches to mean three days. In three days the chief cupbearer would be reinstated to his position, offering wine to Pharaoh again. How did Joseph know the three branches represent three days? No human mind can figure that out this is supernatural wisdom he got concerning the dream.

If we would develop our consciousness to the realities of the spirit most problems of dreams interpretation would be solved. It seems that half of our dreams are self-interpreted by our own spirit man. Our spirit man, the real we in the body knows everything, in the past I had 2 visions and a few dreams where I saw the Lord

Hearing God's voice in Dreams

Jesus, no one introduced Him to me but I supernaturally knew it was Him. There have been many others who also saw Him in visions and dreams whether believers or non-believers and knew it was Him.

The story of the rich man and Lazarus is a great example of this. It is something that truly happened not a parable. In parables Jesus Christ never mentions names. Both the rich man and Lazarus died, Lk. 16:23-24 GW, *"He went to hell, where he was constantly tortured. As he looked up, in the distance he saw Abraham and Lazarus. He yelled, 'Father Abraham! Have mercy on me! Send Lazarus to dip the tip of his finger in water to cool off my tongue. I am suffering in this fire."* We learn here that the rich man in hell saw Abraham, this man was born over 4 000 years after Abraham, there were no cameras nor painters in those days we have today to capture memories or people. He instinctively knew it was Abraham, no one told him it was him but he knew it was him. It could have been anyone, it could have been Isaac or Jacob or David or anyone of the Old Testament great characters.

We have many times dreamt things in our dreams and found answers and interpretations while dreaming. You just know something in the dream supernaturally or understand what the dream means or is about supernaturally. I am therefore convinced that if we develop our spirit man as explored in the previous chapter we would have less interpreting to do.

To the chief wine bearer, he (Joseph) told him Pharaoh was going to restore his position in the kingdom. Joseph urged the chief cupbearer to remember him after being restored. Both Pharaoh's officers were released out of prison and things happened to them according to Joseph's interpretations of their dreams but the chief cupbearer forgot Joseph (Gen. 39-40).

Joseph interpreting the chief baker's dream

When the chief baker learned that his inmate dream interpretation was good he told of his dream:

> *When the chief baker saw that the interpretation was good, he said unto Joseph, I also was in my dream, and, behold, I had three white baskets on my head: And in the uppermost basket there was of all manner of bakemeats for Pharaoh, and the birds did eat them out of the basket upon my head.* (Genesis 40:16-17 KJV).

Let's break the dream according to the P.I.C concept.

- Context: is about three white baskets on the head of the chief baker. The context of the dream is negative as the birds ate the bakes in the upper basket.

- Items: are the three white baskets and all manner of baked goods in the upper basket baked for Pharaoh.

- Persona: the chief baker, birds of the sky, and Pharaoh even if he does not appear in the dream but is only mentioned.

Now let's look at how Joseph interpreted the dream.

> *[18]And Joseph answered and said, this is the interpretation thereof: The three baskets are three days:*
>
> *[19]Yet within three days shall Pharaoh lift thy head from off thee, and shall hang thee on a tree, and the birds shall eat thy flesh from off thee.*

The three baskets are three days. At that time bread only lasted a day after being baked. So three baskets equate to three days. Joseph went on to tell the chief baker that after three days Pharaoh will hang him and the birds of the sky will eat his flesh. Why didn't Joseph interpret a promotion like he did the chief butler? Throughout the Bible, God used wine to represent joy and blessings in a positive context. In a negative context, he used wine to represent gluttony and wantonness. So we can only know which aspect is possible by looking at the context of the dream, is it a positive or a negative dream? Bread is consumed, throughout the Bible bread has only been for consumption. Matthew 26:26 KJV, *"And as they were eating, Jesus took bread, and blessed it, and brake it, and gave it to the disciples, and said, Take, eat; this is my body."*

Jesus only broke the bread but never divided the wine. The bread He broke in the gospel of Luke He said, *"This is my body which is given* (broken) *for you."* He only stops there. He signified by this that in His death His body would die and remain dead. We can only experience God In the death of the flesh, it is meant to die and never surface to life again. In His resurrection He was resurrected with a new and a perfect body, *"Flesh* (bread) *and blood cannot inherit the Kingdom of God."* 1 Cor. 15:50 KJV. Only the resurrection body that has no flesh and blood but is both 100% spiritual and matter can see the Kingdom.

It was a single bread divided into many pieces but the wine was a single wine drank from the same cup also see Lk. 22:19-20, Mar. 14:22-23. The wine (blood) He speaks of it as the New Covenant. His blood not like His flesh speaks better things than the blood of Abel. The word speaks is present in active tense meaning the efficacy of the blood is still effective even at this point. This was the knowledge Joseph had of the mysteries of God. God spoke promotion to the chief butler through wine (redemption) but spoke death to the chief baker through bread (death of the old nature). Another negative aspect that makes us see that the message of the dream is negative is birds, they normally eat dead meats. We deduce therefore that the context is negative.

> Genesis 40:20 KJV emphasis added, *"And it came to pass the third day, which was Pharaoh's birthday that he made a feast unto all his servants: and he lifted the*

head of the chief butler and the chief baker among his servants."

It is also important for us to learn the faithfulness of Joseph to God from the above examples. He did not withdraw from interpreting the truth the same way to both the chief butler and the chief wine baker without feeling he does not want to disappoint the chief baker because his dream seemed negative. This is truly a mark of true stewardship.

Joseph interprets Pharaoh's dreams

Genesis 41:1-7 KJV

> *[1]And it came to pass at the end of two full years (two full years after Joseph interpreted the dreams of the chief butler and the chief baker), that Pharaoh dreamt: and, behold, he stood by the river.*
>
> *[2]And, behold, there came up out of the river seven well-favored kine and fatfleshed; and they fed in a meadow.*
>
> *[3]And, behold, seven other kine came up after them out of the river, ill-favored and leanfleshed; and stood by the other kine upon the brink of the river.*
>
> *[4]And the ill-favored and leanfleshed kine did eat up the seven well-favored and fat kine. So Pharaoh awoke.*
>
> *[5]And he slept and dreamt the second time: and, behold, seven ears of corn came up upon one stalk, rank and good.*
>
> *[6]And, behold, seven thin ears and blasted with the east wind sprung up after them.*

[7]And the seven thin ears devoured the seven rank and full ears. And Pharaoh awoke, and, behold, it was a dream.

If you read through the chapter you will learn that the next morning Pharaoh summoned all his magicians and wise men. After he told them his dream none could interpret them for him. The chief butler then remembered Joseph. He was taken out of prison the Bible lets us know he shaved and put on new clothes, a man of excellence he was. Standing before Pharaoh, the Pharaoh tells him, Genesis 41:15 KJV, *"And Pharaoh said unto Joseph, I have dreamt a dream, and there is none that can interpret it: and I have heard say of thee, that thou canst understand a dream to interpret it."*

You should notice how when he was confronted with these flattery words from Pharaoh which would have gullibly ensnared him to rely on his past experiences of dreams interpretation but Joseph rested on his faith and trust in God to give him the interpretation of those dreams. Genesis 41:16 KJV, *"And Joseph answered Pharaoh, saying, it is not in me: God shall give Pharaoh an answer of peace."* Experience should never precede revelation. We should always rely on and trust God in interpreting dreams. Pharaoh saw the same dream twice but each dream differing from the other. When we dream the same dream repeatedly, it can be at a span of three days or one week. This means this issue is pressing and God wants to draw our attention to it.

Let's continue using the C.I.P concept to look at Joseph's interpretation of Pharaoh's dreams. Beginning with the first dream.

- Context: the dream is about seven fat and good looking cows and seven ugly and gaunt-looking cows. The context is negative since the gaunt and lean cows will devour the seven healthy cows.
- Items: Cows, river, and meadow

- Persona: Cows

This dream falls under the category of the visions of the night. Pharaoh is an observer not a participant in this dream. The negative outcomes predicted by the dream will affect him as much as they will any citizen of Egypt. We know the dream concerns Egypt because the river Nile is Egypt's. As once stipulated at the beginning of this book the source of dreams is God.

If dreams came from demons or call it idols, the Egyptian magicians would have brought the interpretation. When we say no one could interpret Pharaoh's dream we mean none of Egypt's wise men was spot on. According to the Midrash, they interpreted the dream of seven cows to mean he would have seven daughter's and they'd die and the seven healthy-looking heads of grain to mean Pharaoh will conquer seven kingdoms and the seven sun-scorched heads of grain that devoured the former healthy-looking grain to mean that these seven kingdoms will later rebel against Pharaoh. Pharaoh did not accept these interpretations.

When your dream is interpreted right you will sense satisfaction or confirmation in your spirit but when it is wrongly interpreted there will be a sense of uneasiness or unrest in your spirit. Also mind Nebuchadnezzar's dream, not a single one of the magicians or astrologers of Babylon was able to interpret his dream. For Pharaoh, it was until Joseph came that he had the interpretation. For Nebuchadnezzar, it was until Daniel came that he found his interpretation. Both young men expressed faith in God as the dream interpreter.

Egypt and Babylon not only worshipped idols but also worshipped the dead this point is very important for fellow Africans as over 70% are in ancestry worship. Dreams do not come from ancestors because the magi and the astrologers of Babylon would have given the interpretation and in the above-mentioned case of Pharaoh, the wise men and magicians of Egypt would also have. The source of dreams is God. Dreams that come from demons bring fear and oppression. Many Africans are offended at this as they angrily lash out that their ancestors are not demons. Think about this, every dead person is either in hades (hell) if it was a non-believer or in heaven provided he or she was a believer (See Eccl. 9:4-6). There can be no middle ground. God doesn't send the dead to the living He has trillions of angels for that. If you dream of a dead person giving you a message in a dream it can only be a demon masquerading itself as your ancestor. Demons can also masquerade as angels of light (See 2 Cor. 11:14).

Each element of a dream consists of either a negative or positive meaning as said before the context determines the meaning. Here is what the elements of the dream mean, the river Nile where the cows come from represents prosperity and wealth, the Nile was Egypt's source of fertility and wealth. The healthy cows' Pharaoh saw symbolize meat and strength for wealth creation. The gaunt and ugly cows came up and devoured the seven healthy-looking cows. The opposite of abundance and wealth is famine and poverty. The gaunt and ugly cows symbolize famine and want. The skill for dream interpretation calls for simplicity: when cows are thin they are eating less which means there's less food, less food equals famine. The ancients measured the growth of cows in years not in months (See Gen. 15:9) so Joseph knew that the famine was destined for seven years as goes the seven cows.

Pharaoh woke up from his dream. He slept again and dreamt of a second dream. Let us now look into Pharaoh's second dream. The second dream confirmed the first dream.

He saw seven heads of grain coming up from a single stalk. They looked plump and good according to the New King James Version. Then seven thin heads blasted by the east wind sprang up after them. The seven thin heads devoured the seven healthy and goodly looking heads of grain (Gen. 41:5-7). The context of the dream is also negative, it is about a stalk of grain that grows seven good heads of grain and seven bad heads of grain that devour the former. The items are the seven good heads of grain and the bad seven heads of grain and the east wind. In both dreams, the first seven good items are devoured by the second negative items which elucidate to us that the bad season will suddenly interrupt the good season. The nature of the first dream is more concerned about the years of the famine while the second dream is more concerned about the nature of the famine. The cows symbolize meat while the grain symbolizes bread.

Meat and bread were the main life sustenance sources for the aboriginals. By putting the dreams together we have consummated the prediction of the famine and its nature. The second dream deals with the nature of the famine, grain. We have Pharaoh seeing the seven bad heads of grain which appeared after the seven good heads of grain blasted by the eastern wind. The eastern wind was always associated with introducing the famine and worst of times throughout the Bible, Eze. 17:10 GW, *"It might be planted again, but will it live and grow? It will wither completely when the east wind blows on it. It will certainly wither in the garden where it is growing."* Also, see Hos. 13:15 and Jon. 4:8.

Chapter 13

HOW TO INTERPRET DREAMS Pt2

In this study, we will look at certain dreams and how I have interpreted them to give you an in-depth understanding and knowledge of this study. Though some dreams tend to be straight forward needing no interpretation.

Here is an example, before I heeded the call to go into ministry I had been running from it for two years because of fear of failure due to observing certain pastors around my life at the time and I felt I was so young just 24 years old, of course, I still am young. Until I received a message from a dream from Apostle Takudzwa Masunda who became famous by leading a very prominent and powerful Student Christian Movement at Mafikeng University of the North West province of South Africa that was said to attract more than 400 students and became a torch of flame among young people who in turn took the flame back to their communities and attended churches.

We first came into contact when he was invited to minister by a brother of mine a then student at North West University and who was one of his board of directors in the movement who had hosted a two weeks revival in Kagiso. Though the guest Apostle Takudzwa Masunda was to minister only one evening we got to shake hands, chat with him for less than 45 minutes along with the other brothers and we knew each other from there. He never heard me preach before. When he was in Australia with his wife he searched my name on Facebook until he found me and sent me a Facebook friendship request that I accepted. He then told me of a dream he had of me:

Hearing God's voice in Dreams

> *"I had a dream where I saw you teaching ministers, giving them foundational truths of the gospel' in your words, you said, "we are a different generation full of the word and power of God". You will be a household name, many will come to draw from you lessons that will correct a lot of errors that have pervaded the body of Christ.*

The above dream is an example of a dream that needs no interpretation in that it is vivid and straight to the point. I always knew and seen that God has called me for leaders and matters of doctrine. On receiving the dream I was reassured and comforted. I set out to pray for another confirmation from God of which God answered through another dream on the 19th of September 2015. The dreams I feel are more important I write them down in my dream journal. Here is the dream below:

> *I dreamt I was in an unfamiliar place. I took a small Corsa van. According to the dream I had a stepfather and the mother I had isn't the one I know.*

> *All my friends were driving their cars. I was the only one with no driving experience. After I had taken the car to drive it. On my left was seated a young woman I had never seen before. The car went on just immediately upon mounting it. It started before I inserted the key for the ignition. It took off at maximum speed. I tried minimizing the speed but couldn't, the only thing I could do was to control it. It passed all my friends and other cars on the road amazingly I never lost control of it.*

I arrived at my destination. The place seemed like Swaneville (where I previously lived). There was the most amazing structure being built by the government. I was now with Prophet Sam (a certain brother of mine in Christ), it was no longer the young lady I started with. We arrived before all the other cars that were following me. After 3 hours they still hadn't appeared. I heard the Lord's audible voice say, "In blessing, I will surely bless you."

Interpretation: This dream was the confirmation from the Lord after the one I had received from my brother Takudzwa. It dealt with my whole future and reassured me of success when I was afraid to fail in ministry. The dream covers my whole destiny. In it, I had a stepfather and the mother I had is not my real mother. By this time, it was 2015 my mother was still alive. On the following year on February the second week, she would pass on to be with the Lord. The dream was on point in this area too. Do always consider the simplest form of interpreting a symbol, the van symbolizes ministry. There are two types of ministries we have. One is the mainstream ministry, a local church the second is the personal ministry.

Personal ministry is your area of gifting, worshipping, business, arts, professional vocation, etc. The Corsa van is used to carry goods or people from one destination to another. This then symbolizes the mainstream ministry, a local church. I was the one driving the van meaning I am to be the pastor of this local church. In the dream all my friends were driving cars, by 2015 almost most of my brothers and friends in the Lord were not in ministry by this I am not inferring on personal ministry but the mainstream.

The following year October the 23rd was the beginning of my mainstream ministry most of my friends and brothers in the Lord were to begin by 2017 to 2019. As I was driving the van I noticed a young woman I had never seen on my left. I still remember that in the dream I felt a strong connection with the lady, a connection deeper and stronger than that of a friend, I had a knowing this would be my wife. Strangely, by this time I was in the last months of dating with the lady I told about in chapter 10 whom I dreamt, I would not be with in the future. Dreams are so on point. I somehow saw my wife before I even met her in 2016 December the 26th. The car was cruising at a great speed that I tried to slow down but it didn't, surprisingly I could control it. This reveals my success and effortless leadership in mainstream ministry and the acceleration I'd experience.

I finally arrived at my destination. The place seemed like Swaneville where I lived before. By the time of this dream, I was permanently living in Kagiso. Where I arrived there was the most amazing structure being built by the government. The government means God. I was by that time in the dream with a brother of mine in the Lord Prophet Sam, it was not any longer the young lady I started with. This means in the early days of my ministry the person who will play a major role will be my wife.

When someone is seated on the seat next to the driver's it normally means the pastor's assistant. So toward the course of the end of my calling God will provide me with someone to assist me in ministry who will also play a major role. This individual will enhance a prophet's office. We arrived at the destination before all the other cars that we passed on the way. I arrived 3 hours before the rest of the cars and before my friends. Three is the God number this meaning that it's God who will be doing this, the timing of my arrival to my purposed destination and then I heard the Lord's audible voice say to me, "In blessing, I will surely bless you." This dream is more about the Lord exhorting me that in my going into ministry He will be the one more in control than I will be and that my finishing is all in His strength not in mine.

I immediately agreed to go into the ministry that which I feared going into ministry in my strength and terms was resolved by the Lord. Our Lord is most amazing and all gracious. He calls you to do He will give you strength for and He will be your comforter all through the way. His faithfulness is priceless and His love is unrelenting.

The Chickenpox dream

> *Today I dreamt I was home and the light of my living room didn't want to switch on and I switched it on and off and on and it switched on, the globe had water in it and when it switched on the water started to boil and I said to my son he must be careful because the light might explode because of water. Then a boy from our street came in complaining he has chickenpox. Then another person came complaining about chickenpox. A lot of people came then I asked my cousin, she said she also has chickenpox. Then one person said it will come to your family and I said never, it will not come near me and my family. I started to confess good health for me and my family. As we were going to the front I saw a choir dressed in yellow and black and then on the one side I saw a lot of people with chickenpox then I woke up. For two nights I dreamt of wearing black and gold garments. Then I heard a voice saying from now on as you preach wear black it's the new prophetic color for this hour.*
>
> *-Thaps*

Interpretation: your home where you live, this is your current situation. The light: there is a way or solution you desire. It is in your power not dependent on someone else's. But the more you reach for it you fail every time. When finally it lights the water inside boils. This means your attempt to solve your current situation has tests and trials along with it. People might turn against you, you might lose friends and be persecuted. Three people from your neighborhood came with cases of chickenpox. Meaning God is revealing to you a situation that will attack the people you know (sort of a disease) and bring fear to them (This was during the time of the Corona pandemic). The Lord is encouraging you to continue steadfast in the confession of the Word.

In front of you, you saw a choir wearing yellow and black. Yellow means a group of people in your life, this might be a prayer group or those leading you taken by thoughts of fear and ignorance of the ways of the Lord. The other side is people near you attacked by a certain infirmity. The color black carried no positive meaning in the Scriptures. What it means is the work of the enemy, darkness, or ignorance. This means you are beginning to accept things you weren't supposed to, some of those things you take as to mean spiritual things. Slowly you might be vulnerable to lose spiritual values. This is both a warning and a prophetic dream. Confessions of Scriptures and meditations will help you. Do also pray for people around your life.

The Red car dream

Hi Apostle I dreamt of driving a red car and I also saw so and so (the brother had just started into ministry and they were both trying to start a relationship with the lady that sent me the dream) *driving a red car too but the models were different. His was a brand new AMG Mercedes and Mine was my actual car then I saw that I was not driving my car I was in the back seat but I then immediately asked why am I sitting at the back of my car instead of the front seat...I then jumped over to the front seat and started driving it, funny enough I saw my grandmother right next to the driver's seat not talking just relaxed. I then noticed that my side mirrors of the car are damaged, one was even broken. On the other side I just saw so and so's car moving straight with a slow but steady motion. I then woke up*

-Anonymous

Interpretation: A car speaks of ministry, the color red in this context is both your callings and anointing. They are different, meaning your ministries are different (by then I did not know they were into each other and working on building a relationship, the Holy Spirit was revealing to the lady that they had two separate ministries by such means their relationship would not work which is what later happened). You haven't taken control over your assignment. God is bringing you to a point of taking over your assignment and at that moment you will realize that there was a certain principle of old that was governing your life and assignment. The driver, faceless men in your car is the Holy Spirit which in this aspect is not bad. Side mirrors are your ministry foundations (mirror being the Word according to James 1:23-24), they are your governing principles or foundational doctrines.

In her own words, she confirmed by saying, *"It is true that I have had foundational errors in terms of doctrine."*

Giving an Offering dream

In 2015 God told me my ministry work in Kagiso will not be longer than 5 years. I knew this would depend on my level of obedience to God. Mind you, this was before 2016 the year of beginning ministry in Kagiso. The morning of this dream was 30 October 2020 just after the previous Sunday of the 25th when I had announced to the church that God had told my wife and me it is time to move to another area God had revealed to us to start another work of ministry. My wife had woken up with a dream during level 5 of the Covid 19, she saw me handing over my crown and kingship garment to one of my young pastors. According to the dream we were inside the church as I did this, before everyone.

After a month or so I had a confirming dream and then shortly afterward it was followed by another. And just the week when we were to resume our church gatherings after the Covid 19 pandemic lockdown we were in level 1. I was with Pastor Mario at Kagiso mall when we were met by prophet Obed Reign. He had met me a year ago and told me he has a message for me. I lost his contacts and we met again. He said the same thing again, concerning having a message for me. He arranged to visit our church.

Two weeks later he came and after the service, he asked to see my wife and me. He confirmed things we knew concerning our calling and ministry and then confirmed the issue of opening another branch somewhere and the type of ministry partners God will send us. We knew our leaving Kagiso will be soon but we planned to stay until maybe the following year which would be 2021 and leave around October. Unbeknownst to me was that in the following weeks I'd feel spiritual unrest and absence of peace when I continued ministering. After a lot of prayer and consideration, I finally accepted my work as done in Kagiso then we handed over the reins of the ministry to my assistant pastor. I then felt the rest and peace I needed in the following work after this doing. The following dream took place at a moment when I had been deeply meditating on my next move in ministry.

I woke up with a dream at 3:57 am. In this dream, I was leading a church. It was in a big hall so full of young people. In my heart, it was like it was the church I am currently leading now. It was time to give the offering. I went up front to give. On reaching for my pocket I had one 10 rands. It was supposed to be two of them. The other one I gave it for offering when we were outside of the premises and the one I had left I felt I had spared it for transport. So I turned back disappointed since there was no extra one to give. People were taking envelopes in front and putting R10s for the offering.

Zama came to where I was standing at the back and put her hands around my neck and placed five R2s in my shirt pocket. I thought she saw me trying to offer. I then proceeded up front to give it. Upfront there were offering attendants clad in dignity.

When I arrived it was written R999 I felt it was short of 10 rands to make R1000. I pulled out four R2s, Zama told me I had a 1 rand left. Her hands still around my neck. I pulled it out too and it was R2. I offered a complete 10 rand made up of silver five R2s. I felt blessings being released over my life as I gave the R10. In the dream, I felt and addressed Zama as my cousin. After I gave the offering the offering attendants restrained anyone from coming to add as the money was now balanced.

Interpretation: This dream is about the current ministry. The R999 offered is the will of the people in the ministry. The five 2 rands which make up an R10 I was given by my cousin lady in the dream speak of been given a special grace (five means grace), a grace to obey and carry out the task given to me (R10). My cousin sister had her hands over my shoulders, this represents the Holy Spirit taking control over my life and enabling me to lead well and make the right decisions. The cousin sister being the Holy Spirit in this context. My offering of the R10 means my surrendering to the Lord's leading and well as I am being empowered by the Holy Spirit to do so. The last R2 I was told was an R1 speaks of 2 becoming 1 which means unity, this also points back to my being one with God's will. One is the number of God the Father, see Numbers in Dreams.

According to the dream I only needed to give R10 for the money to be an R1000 and when I had given the money it was written down and no one else was allowed to add so to keep the amount balanced as strictly an R1000. This means for the ministry I am currently leading in Kagiso to reach the will of God (R1000) now that God has everyone's will (R999) it only needed my part of obedience and submission, which will of God will, in turn, be a blessing to the ministry (Kagiso) as a whole and my life personally.

PART II: DREAM BIBLE

Symbols of Life and Death in Dreams

Ecclesiastes 12:3-7 GW

3. Remember your Creator when those who guard the house tremble, strong men are stooped over, the women at the mill stop grinding because there are so few of them, and those who look out of the windows see a dim light.

4. Remember your Creator when the doors to the street are closed, the sound of the mill is muffled, you are startled at the sound of a bird, and those who sing songs become quiet.

5. Remember your Creator when someone is afraid of heights and dangers along the road, the almond tree blossoms, the grasshopper drags itself along, and the caper bush has no fruit. Mortals go to their eternal rest, and mourners go out in the streets.

6. Remember your Creator before the silver cord is snapped, the golden bowl is broken, the pitcher is smashed near the spring, and the water wheel is broken at the cistern.

7. Then the dust of mortals goes back to the ground as it was before, and the breath of life goes back to God who gave it.

We will use the above excerpt to reveal these symbols

Symbolism for a decaying body

Verses 3 to 5 of the above chapter represent a decaying human body. The *"guard or guardians"* speak of arms, *"strong men"* is the legs, *"women who grind"* is the teeth (remembering the New Testament consistent allegory of the grinding of teeth), *"those who look"* are the eyes, *"the doors"* are lips (the Hebrew is dual as representing what we call "folding doors"), *"daughters of songs"* mourning voices, *"the almond tree blossoms"* this is the white hair of old age, *"grasshopper drags itself along"* the stiffness of movement due to old age, *"the capper bush has no fruit"* strengthless, no more productivity.

Vs. 3 strong men stooped over (effects produced by terror), guardians of the house tremble (one of the effects produced by the loss of life), women stop grinding at the mill, those who look out of the window see dim lights. Any of the preceding pictures seen in a dream foretell death. *Those who look out of the window see dim lights* this represents death in your own family or extended family since in the dream you have to be inside the house to see dim light outside the window. Dreaming inside the house speaks of anything that happens around you, e.g. your family or extended family.

Symbols of Life and Death

Remember your Creator before the silver cord is snapped, the golden bowl is broken, the pitcher is smashed near the spring, and the water wheel is broken at the cistern. (Eccl. 12: 6 GW).

The above verse reveals the dissolution of the human spirit from the human body. Remember that we are tripartite beings: spirit, soul, and body, refer to the 11th chapter. We are spirits that have a soul, living inside a body.

"Remember your Creator before the silver cord is snapped, the golden bowl is broken" to effectively expound this portion of Scripture it is needful we first explain the golden bowl before we attempt to explain the silver cord. The golden bowl spoken of here is the same one spoken of in Zechariah 4 verses 3 to 4. The golden bowl was a vessel or reservoir used in the Old Testament tabernacle and later in the temple of Solomon. On top of it sat the Menorah (the golden seven-branched candlestick) from which the oil flowed into

Hearing God's voice in Dreams

the lamps. The symbolism of the lamp is life. Someone once wrote, *"It can scarcely remain doubtful then that the "golden bowl" is life as manifested through the material fabric of man's body."* In those days houses and temples lit lamps on top of the bowl and had the bowl hang by a chain (silver cord). *"When we wish to keep the lamp burning, we take care to supply it with oil."* (Plutarch, *Pericles*.) So Plato (*de Legg*. p. 776). As stipulated above, a lamp represents life—when the silver cord (chain) that holds the golden bowl which holds the lamp snaps *"the lamp of life finally falls with a crash on the floor"* F. B Meyer. And the golden bowl breaks that represents an eternal disintegration of the human spirit from the body, death. Dreaming of a smashed pitcher, and a water wheel broken at the cistern, dreaming of such foretells death.

More symbols of life and death in dreams

Here is a great example of life in a dream, let's say a pregnant lady dreams of buying two buckets of water. This means she is pregnant with twins because a bucket of water represents life and if they are two it represents two lives. Here are more examples below of life and death in dreams:

- Dreaming losing your loved one and you cry in the dream. Example: you dream of losing your father or mother to death and you cry so much in the dream or even cry to a point that you wake up crying from the dream. Such dreams may be direct you might have to pray for that loved one, in the case of your father pray for your father in the case of your mother pray for your mother and break the spirit of death. Many times when you wake up listen to your spirit (heart) or recall what your intuition was telling you in the dream this is very important since it many times lets you know that your dream is direct or not, if you still not

Hearing God's voice in Dreams

sure go ahead and pray for the person revealed in the dream, refer to chapter 10 of this book *How to stop bad dream predictions.*
- Dreaming of blood represents life when blood is spilled it represents death.
- Dreaming of a cup of water or oil represents life when it breaks it represents death.
- Dreaming of a chain represents life and when it breaks it represents death.
- Dreaming of a bucket of water represents life when it breaks it represents death.
- Dreaming of a pitcher with water or near a fountain represents life when the pitcher breaks it represents death.
- Dreaming of a wheel of a cistern on a cistern represents life when it breaks it represents death.
- Dreaming of a plant on the ground represents life when the plant is uprooted it represents death.
- Dreaming of a garment represents life and when it is old it means the coming of age, old age and when it is eaten by a moth in a dream this represents gradual death.
- Dreaming of light represents life when you dream gross darkness it represents death.
- Dreaming of a morgue foretells death, sometimes it means a ministry that condemns people or that preaches the law of death.
- Dreaming of an open grave foretells death.
- Dreaming of a scorpion reveals the spirit of death.
- Dreaming of a green horse reveals the spirit of death (the Bible calls this color pale see

Revelation chapter 6 verse 8 *"for it is used constantly of the paleness of the human face when terror-struck, or dead or dying."* – Cambridge Bible).

- Dreaming of a venomous serpent reveals the spirit of death (the angel of death in 1 Corinthians 10:10 is called the destroyer which is the Greek *olothreutes* specifically meaning a venomous serpent).

Numbers

Remember my statement: the greatest thing I learned about God through His Word is that He is very intentional and very detailed as a result every detail in Scripture is by deliberate design. The colors, the numbers, even the measurements of the Tabernacle and its vessels, the description of certain garments are all placed there perfectly by the hand of the Holy Spirit without a single contradiction and each holds a specific and an intended message.

Below you will learn both the positive and the negative sides of each number.

One

Positive: unity, as the first number it is also the number of God, He is the beginning and is always the author of all things. Originally the Old Testament was written in Hebrew, the Hebrew languages have no numerals, and the letters are used for numerals. One is the first Hebrew letter alpha, the letter is a pictograph of a bull's head which represents chieftaincy, leadership, the head of household, a father. All these are the characters of God. *"Hear, O Israel: The LORD our God is one LORD."* Deu. 6:4 KJV. Rightly translated the one used here is *echad* not *kole* meaning the Lord is one in unity since He is three in One.

Negative: that which claims independence from God, rebellion.

Two

Positive: witness, testimony (2 Cor. 13:1), union, marriage (Gen. 2:24), help (Ecc. 4:9). This number throughout the Scriptures also reveals the work or the presence of the Lord Jesus. In the Old Testament, it reveals the Lord Jesus before His incarnation, *"And the angel of the LORD called to Abraham a second time from heaven and said, "By myself I have sworn, declares the LORD, because you have done this and have not withheld your son, your only son, I will surely bless you, and I will surely multiply your offspring as the stars of heaven and as the sand that is on the seashore. And your offspring shall possess the gate of his enemies, and in your offspring shall all the nations of the earth be blessed, because you have obeyed my voice."* Gen. 22:15-18 ESV.

The Angel of the Lord having called out to Abraham from heaven twice was the Lord before His incarnation. Later in the book of Hebrews we read that the Angel was God, *"For God, having promised to Abraham, since he had no greater to swear by, swore by himself, saying, surely blessing I will bless thee, and multiplying I will multiply thee."* Heb. 6:13-14 Darby.

Every time the Angel of the Lord is mentioned in Scriptures remember that that was the Lord Jesus before His incarnation. 1Sa. 3:10 ASV, *"And Jehovah came, and stood, and called as at other times, Samuel, Samuel. Then Samuel said, Speak; for thy servant heareth."* The calling twice of Samuel reveals the work of God the Son before His incarnation. Let us now see in the New Testament, Joh. 1:51 ESV, *"And he* (Jesus) *said to him, "Truly, truly, I say to you, you will see heaven opened, and the angels of God ascending and descending on the Son of Man."* King James has it, *"Verily, verily."* The word represents the Hebrew "Amen, amen" as the Douay-Rheims Bible has it. Jesus used two amen each one representing the member of the Godhead, God the Father, and God the Holy Spirit. They can't be three since the speaker Jesus cannot testify of Himself but the other two members of the Godhead can testify of the statements He made in His earthly ministry.

Negative: division or the work of the enemy. God sent Moses and Aaron to deliver His people out of Egypt they were opposed by Jannes and Jambres (see 2 Tim. 3:8), Exo. 7:22 GW, *"But the Egyptian magicians did the same thing using their magic spells. So Pharaoh continued to be stubborn and would not listen to Moses and Aaron, as the LORD had predicted."*

Three

Positive: the number of the Godhead (God the Father, God the Son, and God the Holy Spirit), resurrection (Jesus died for three days and three nights).

Negative: denial, Peter denied Christ three times, temptation, Jesus was tempted three times, Adam and Eve were tempted in three areas, 1Joh 2:16 KJV, *"For all that is in the world, (1) the lust of the flesh, (2) and the lust of the eyes, (3) and the pride of life, is not of the Father, but is of the world."* Emphasis added. Opposition against God (the three characteristics of the Revelation 13 beast, vs 2, *"The beast that I saw was like a leopard. Its feet were like bear's feet. Its mouth was like a lion's mouth."* GW.

Four

Positive: the Gospel (book of Matthew, Mark, Luke, and John), Creation (the four living creatures in heaven, Rev. 4:6), whole wide world (four compass directions, north, east, west, and south), Christ, Dan 3:25 KJV, *"He answered and said, Lo, I see four men lose, walking in the midst of the fire, and they have no hurt; and the form of the fourth is like the Son of God."*

Negative: the world, the world's kingdoms (four beasts of Daniel 7 that represent the world's kingdoms and Nebuchadnezzar's dream of four kingdoms in Daniel 2), satanic nature (the four characteristics of Daniel 7 beasts).

Five

Positive: the completed work of Christ, in the Old Testament, were five offerings Jesus became all of them (grace). Jesus' Name or work (Jesus is a Greek name derived from the Hebrew name Yeshua which is made up of five Hebrew letters).

Negative: Man's responsibility to God (1 plus 4 equals 5, one is the number of the independent God four is the number of the created man thus five is man's responsibility to God).

Hearing God's voice in Dreams

Six

Positive: the number of man (Adam and Eve were created on the sixth day), day (hours of the day are six).

Negative: a man in union with the devil, the number 666 is the number of the antichrist which is a number of a man, Rev. 13:18, the number also means man's efforts and his works, toil, sweat (by the Torah man ought to work six days).

Seven

Positive: perfection, completion, rest (on the seventh day of creation after God had completed everything He rested, the seventh day of the week is hallowed, the seventh year (Shemitah) in the Old Testament was hallowed). Throughout Scriptures, the number seven represents a work of perfection or entering into perfect rest.

Negative: judgment (seven seals judgments, seven trumpets judgments, seven bowls judgments, throughout the books of Revelation we see God's perfect judgments released).

Eight

Positive: resurrection (Jesus was resurrected on the first day of the week, the eighth day), cleansing, consecration (the leper was cleansed on the eighth day), a new beginning (David was the eighth son of Jesse and out of him has initiated a new nation of Israel), salvation (Noah was the eighth person and he entered the ark with seven of his family he was the eighth), covenant (the Old Testament males were circumcised, initiated into Abraham's covenant on the eighth day following birth).

Negative: fat, plumpness, lusty, slippery, greasy, detestable, unethical, indecent from the Hebrew root *shamen*.

Nine

Positive: gifts of the Holy Spirit (1 Cor. 12:8-10), fruits of the born again human spirit (Gal. 5:22-23), innate gifts, potential, expecting to birth out something beautiful (9 months of pregnancy).

Negative: Judgment, the wrath of God (God delivered 10 plagues to the Egyptians, the 10th is set aside as a special case which leaves a total of 9 plagues. They are divided into 3 categories, the first 3 attacks the comfort of Egypt, the next three attack their possessions, and the last three bring out death and destruction), deception, trickery (the Hebrew numeral for 9 is *tet* a pictogram of a curled serpent).

Ten

Positive: the number of the Church (5 wise brides and 5 foolish brides make up 10, Mat. 25, the woman with ten pieces of silver, Lk. 15:8-10), responsibility before God (the ten servants who received ten pounds from the Lord, Lk. 19:12-26, i.e. the tithe), work and walk of obligation (ten fingers and ten toes), the manifestation of Christ and the Holy Spirit (after His resurrection Christ appeared 10 times to His disciples, the disciples waited for 10 days in Jerusalem before receiving the Holy Spirit), obedience to God, the fullness of God's judgment (10 plagues).

Negative: legalism (the Ten Commandments, in the New Testament we are only given two commandments, Joh. 13:34-35, Rom. 13:8-10), persecution and tribulation (the church of Smyrna had tribulation for 10 days, Rev. 2:10), the power of the nations (ten toes represented in Dan. 2, and the ten horns represented in Rev. 17:12).

Eleven

Positive: divine separation, divine mystery (the eleven curtains of the Tabernacle, Exo. 26:8), the word is also made up of the Hebrew word *esheth* meaning fabric or bright.

Negative: incomplete election, incomplete governance (Joseph dreamt eleven stars bowing before him, he being the twelfth, after His resurrection the Lord Jesus was left with eleven apostles after the twelfth apostle Judas Iscariot had committed suicide). *"Brothers, what the Holy Spirit predicted through David in Scripture about Judas had to come true. Judas led the men to arrest Jesus. With the money he received from the wrong he had done, he bought a piece of land where he fell headfirst to his death. His body split open, and all his internal organs came out. You've read in Psalms, 'Let his home be deserted, and let no one live there,' and 'Let someone else take his position.'" "Therefore, someone must be added to our number to serve with us as a witness that Jesus came back to life."* Acts 1: 16, 18 & 20 GW.

Twelve

Positive: governance (Mat. 26:53), Israel (Gen. 37:5-11, 49:28, Lk. 22:30, Rev. 12:1-5), day (Joh. 11:9), Kingdom (In the first half of the book of Revelation number 7 is more prominent but in the second half of the book number 12 becomes more prominent, 12 thousand sealed in each tribe of Israel, 12 gates, 12 pearls, 12 angels, 12 foundations, 12 names of the apostles, the tree of life bearing 12 different fruits, etc.).

Negative: servitude (Gen. 14:3-4 GW, *"The five kings joined forces and met in the valley of Siddim (that is, the Dead Sea). For 12 years they had been subject to Chedorlaomer, but in the thirteenth year they rebelled."*).

Thirteen

Positive: Jesus as a burnt offering pleasing to the Father (on the feast of Succoth which was on the 15 days of the Jewish seven month the Israelites were to offer 13 young bullocks), echad (one in unity), a fountain of living water, building (Solomon built his house for thirteen years), priestly inheritance (upon Israel arriving in Canaan the Levites were given thirteen cities, Jos. 21:19).

Negative: flesh (Ishmael compared to Isaac was a type of the flesh he was circumcised at 13, Gen. 17:25, Isaac was circumcised the 8th day from birth as a type of the promise, see Gal. 4:22-31), rebellion (Gen. 14:3-4 GW, *"The five kings joined forces and met in the valley of Siddim (that is, the Dead Sea). For 12 years they had been subject to Chedorlaomer, but in the thirteenth year they rebelled."*).

Fourteen

Positive: double perfection (7 multiplied by 7, fourteen lambs were to be offered on the Feast of Succoth, see Num. 29:12-13. Solomon made seven days and seven days feast, fourteen days, see 1 Ki. 8:65, the altar of burnt offering in the millennial Kingdom will be 14 cubits long and 14 broad in the four squares thereof, see Eze. 43:17), multiplied blessing, restoration (Job had 7 000 sheep and goats in the beginning in his later years he had 14 000 sheep and goats, see Job 42:12), generations (from Abraham to David are 14 generations; and from David until the carrying away into Babylon are 14 generations, from the carrying away into Babylon unto Christ are 14 generations, see Mat 1:17), beloved, darling, favored (fourteen is the numerical value of the Hebrew letters forming the name of David which means beloved), the hand of God, open hand.

Negative: working for the system, a job (Jacob worked for Laban 14 years in Mesopotamia, according to Gen. 10:10 KJV, *"And the beginning of his* (Nimrod) *kingdom was Babel, and Erech, and Accad, and Calneh, in the land of Shinar."* Babel here is Babylon, according to this verse Babylon is in the land of Shinar, Shinar is the Hebrew word meaning a country of two rivers in Greek the word is Mesopotamia, *Mesos,* meaning *middle,* and *potamos* meaning *river.* Mesopotamia, therefore, means 'between the rivers'. By this, we conclude Jacob was in Babylon. Somewhere in the book, we mention Egypt as the world but Babylon as the system, in this case, Jacob as an employee of the system.).

Fifteen

Positive: the presence, cherubim, God's standard of holiness (in the temple inside the Holy of holies were cherubim above the mercy seat of the Ark of the Covenant 10 cubits high which was 15 feet high, see 1 Ki. 6:26, the molten sea in the temple was 15 feet in diameter, this is where the priests washed their hands and feet), the Blessing (Numbers 6:22-27, the *Shema*, the priestly blessing is made up of 15 Hebrew words), to ascend (each of the fifteen Psalms 120 to 134 is entitled 'A Song of Ascents' see the RSV and the NIV. These were psalms sang by worshippers from the country areas as they made their journey to Jerusalem for the various annual festivals.).

Negative: 5 by 3 bring 15, 5 can also stand for the conditions of the created, remember David picking up 5 smooth stones against Goliath and his four brothers who were the offspring of giants and 3 is the God number. Here, 15 enunciates the condition of creation before God, the condition of creation is currently under the fall, evil, wicked and unholy (the 5 champions of the Philistines, Goliath, and his four brothers, the half-human and half angelic breed, see Gen. 6:4).

Sixteen

Positive: look, with you (God), love (the 13th Chapter of first Corinthians mentions 16 attributes of the God-kind of love).

Negative: human kind of love, affection, selfishness, self-glorification, boasting.

Seventeen

Positive: sacrifice, well, repossession, restoration of property (Jer. 32:9 KJV, *"And I bought the field of Hanameel my uncle's son, that was in Anathoth, and weighed him the money, even seventeen shekels of silver.* The Lord spoke to Jeremiah when he was in prison to buy his uncle's son's land. The Lord affirmed this deed as proving that Israel after the Babylon captivity will come back to repossess their land, see vs. 15), beginning of destiny or calling (the Bible specifically details that Joseph was 17 when he began to dream and being hated of his brothers, remember every number in Scripture is by deliberate design).

Negative: premature, short-lived, untimely (the Bible states that Rehoboam, Solomon's son reigned 17 years in Judah because he displeased the Lord his reign was short, see 1 Ki. 14:21, Jehoahaz, the king of Isreal did evil before the Lord, thus, his reign over the kingdom of Israel was short-lived, he only reigned 17 years, see 2 Ki. 13:1-2, Jacob lived the remainder of his years in Egypt, it was short-lived 17 years, see Gen. 47:28).

Eighteen

Positive: life, living (*Chay* the Hebrew word for life is the numerical value for 18).

Negative: sin, fallen.

Nineteen

Positive: faith, obtaining the inheritance and the promises (in the book of Hebrews 11 we have a mention of nineteen names of the Old Testament patriarchs in connection to faith)

Negative: the opposite of faith is unbelief, doubt, walking by the senses.

Twenty

Positive: purchase price, redemption (Joseph was sold to the Ishmaelites for 20 pieces of silver, the book of Ruth a story of redemption has 20 names in it, the Tabernacle had 20 boards on the south and 20 boards on the north, see Exo. 26:18,20, the south side represented Reuben a man, and the northern side represented Dan an eagle. Our redeemer took upon Him two natures to redeem us, the nature of a man (Reuben) and the nature of God (Dan, eagle). When Moses took a census of the people God commanded every man above the age of 20 to bring out ransom money, see Exo. 30:11-16. Young's Literal Translation calls it the atonement money. Atonement means covering that is what the animal blood did in the Old Testament, each year their sins were covered in the New Testament we are introduced to a new word remission of sins, see Mat. 26:28, Rom. 3:25, Heb. 10:18. Number 20 thus means total and once for all redemption has come to us through the blood of Jesus. 20 also means deliverance (Samson a type of Christ judged Israel for 20 years, see Jdg. 15:16 & 20.).

Negative: oppression (The king of the Canaanites, Jabin oppressed Israel for 20 years, see Jdg. 4:1-3. Jacob spent 20 years in Mesopotamia serving Laban, see Gen. 31:38. 1Sa 7:2 GW, *"A long time passed after the ark came to stay at Kiriath Jearim. For 20 years the entire nation of Israel mournfully sought the LORD."*).

The Meaning of Numbers in Hebrew

The following is known as Gematria, *"It is also considered as Gematria when Biblical numbers — for instance, dimensions of buildings are expressed in letters, and words again made of them."* – Cyclopedia Dictionary. Cabala (2). Hebrew has no numerals it is only made up of 22 letters. The same letters also form numbers apart from being words, for example, the Hebrew word for life is *Chay* which can also be number 18. Another example can be found in our previous explanation of number 14, the word beloved *(David)* in the Hebrew can also be number 14. Easily put, numbers are words in Hebrew:

Twenty-One: Vision

Twenty-Two: Hooks, grace, the cross, and cycle

Twenty Three: Rest

Twenty Four: Elder's, (The Twenty-Four Elders only appear in the book of Revelation. The word Elders in Rev. 4 is the Greek *presbuteros*, meaning, the selected, chosen, called out ones. The word for called out ones is where we find the word Church, *Ecclesia*, *"...and I can guarantee that on this rock I will build My Church* (Greek *Ecclesia*). *And the gates of hell will not overpower it,"* (Mat 16:18 GW). The Twenty-Four Elders are the raptured Church around the Throne of God in Heaven. 24 is made up of two twelves, this being the full Church of Jesus Christ, one 12 representing the Jewish believers and the second 12 representing the gentile believers for more on this see my book The Prophecy).

Twenty-Five: Be

Twenty-Six: YHWH (The name Jehovah).

Twenty Seven: Pure

Twenty-Eight: Mire

Twenty Nine: Planted, placed

Thirty: Praised shall be, it also means ministry or fullness of time (in the Old Testament no one was supposed to enter into the service of the Temple until at age 30. The Lord Jesus began His ministry at 30). The least blessing (thirtyfold. See Mat. 4:8).

Thirty-One: El (unto you) the name of God

Thirty-Two: Heart

Forty: Spring of the Torah (Word), preparation (40 days and nights of the flood, 40 years of wandering in the wilderness, 40 days Moses in mount Sinai, 40 days of Jesus' fasting, 40 days from conception to the initial formation of the fetus, 40 weeks of gestation until birth, 40 years of age before a man develops insight).

Forty-Two: Troubled

Fifty-Two: Son

Fifty-Seven: Altar

Sixty: Average blessing (sixtyfold, see Mat. 4:8), maturity, retirement (the priests retired from the office at age 60).

Sixty One: Captive, prisoner

Sixty Two: Between

Seventy-One: Fill, fulfill, and lift

Seventy-Six: Servant

Seventy-Two: Crossing over

Eighty-Two: Fade

Eighty-Five: Diamond

Ninety-One: Messenger, Angel

Ninety-Two: Defiled, sorrows

100: Abundance, the fullness of Blessing (hundredfold, see Mat. 4:8)

110: It means with

120: Chosen

207: Light

271: Pregnant or pregnancy

283: Seed

300: Election by grace, predestination (see, Jdg. 7, the 300 men God chose with Gideon)

360: Eternity, infinity, full circle, a full turn around (revolution)

400: Average length of a nation before it comes to an end

441: Truth

501: Witch, head

999: Man's will apart from God's will (This one is an exception, this meaning doesn't come from the Hebrew meaning but is based on revelation).

1000: Millennium, the Kingdom, the will of God.

Colors

This is a noteworthy saying, every element in dreams has both the positive and the negative side, notably, colors, numbers, and animals. How we know is based on the context of the dream refer to chapter 12.

N.B we will also look at how we generally associate certain colors with emotions, remember that God uses a language that we are well affiliated with, our general concepts to communicate with us. Apart from the biblical side of what colors mean they can also reveal your present moods or the mood of the person dreamt about. Trusting in the Holy Spirit will help you arrive at that conclusion. But in most cases, a person's t-shirt or any inner upper cloth reveals that an example, a yellow t-shirt means feeling joyful and a blue t-shirt means feeling saddened. The color of lower clothes reveals your current experience, example yellow pants from a positive standpoint reveal your joyful walk of faith or we can say you are about to or currently embarking on a joyful journey. The color of shoes on the other hand reveals your type of calling.

White

Positive: calling, purity, sanctification (Isa. 1:18, Rev. 3:4), that which is heavenly (Mat. 17:2, Joh. 20:12), wisdom and strength (Rev. 1:14, Dan. 7:9).

Negative: self-righteousness, human effort (Isa. 64:6, Lev. 13:13).

Red

Positive: salvation, anointing, victory, the blood of Christ, covenant, priesthood (Exo. 25:5, Jos. 2:18-19).

Negative: destruction, sin, rebellion (Isa. 1:18, Rev. 12:3).

Emotion: bold, power, excitement, and energy on the negative it means anger.

Pink

Positive: This color is a combination of red and white when interpreting do refer to red and white depending on whether the dream is positive or negative, it means favor, and it can also mean the love and compassion of Christ.

Negative: It can mean selfishness, self-pity, self-appointed, self-approval.

Emotion: pink represents the passions of childhood while flesh pink represents fear.

Brown

Positive: nurturing, compassion, sustenance, soft spot.

Negative: dry spot, earthly, fleshly

Black

Positive: shrouded by divine mystery, hidden by God (2 Sam. 22:12, Psa. 18:11).

Negative: the works of the enemy, spiritual blindness, ignorance, unawareness (Acts. 26:18, Eph. 5:11). Dreaming of someone wearing black clothes can mean a need to pray for that individual's family since that can also imply death.

Blue

Positive: Revelation, Scripture (Num. 15:38), heavenly, communion (Exo. 24:10, 26:31, Num. 4:7, 9).

Negative: fierce, the Hebrew root of the word is *shachal* meaning the characteristic roar of a lion, according to John Paul Jackson it also means emotional load.

Emotion: trust, strength, dependable on the negative it means sadness.

Purple

Positive: authority, might, kingship, governance, honor (Eze. 23:6, Mk 15:17).

Negative: autocratic, totalitarian, dictatorship, independence.

Emotion: creative, wise, imaginative.

Grey

Positive: Is made up of equal amounts of black and white it means gentle, bland, pleasant, quality, and moderate.

Negative: that which is harsh, severe, violent, disagreeable, lukewarm, poor quality, stingy, frugal, inexpensive, and impressionable (susceptible, English Dictionary: capable of receiving impressions, emotional).

Emotion: neutral, calm, balanced.

Orange

Positive: blessing, fortunate, happiness, goodwill, fruitfulness, increase or perseverance (the Hebrew word for Asher which means blessing was represented by an orange stone on the High Priest's breastplate), Gen. 30:13 Darby, *"And Leah said, Happy am I; for the daughters will call me blessed! and she called his name Asher."*

Negative: the opposite of blessing is a curse, bad will, and troubles, unhappy or stubbornness.

Emotion: friendly, cheerful, confident.

Yellow

Positive: being shepherded, provided for (fed), led, the care taken.

Hearing God's voice in Dreams

Negative: Gen. 49:27 Darby, *"Benjamin— as a wolf will he tear to pieces; in the morning he will devour the prey, And in the evening he will divide the booty."* The Hebrew word wolf used in this verse and throughout the Bible is *ze'eb* it's from an unused root meaning to be yellow. Yellow, therefore, means economic greed, ravenous, to tear apart, predator (the devil), lust, false prophets or false teachers. Biblically the opposite of wolf is the Shepherd (Christ's leadership) as seen in the positive meaning of yellow.

Emotion: optimism, warmth, clarity, hunger. It also is a color of joy.

Green

Positive: prosperity, peace, calm, rest, abundance (Psa. 23:2) or hope. If you have been praying, asking God concerning a decision you are willing to take in your life and you dream in your car and before you is a green traffic light this means God is giving you a go-ahead. Green can also mean a go-ahead.

Negative: envy, luring, enticing, seductive, Gen 13:10 CEV, *"This happened before the LORD had destroyed the cities of Sodom and Gomorrah. And when Lot looked around, he saw there was plenty of water in the Jordan Valley. To Zoar, the valley was as green as the garden of the LORD or the land of Egypt."*

Emotion: peaceful, growth, health, and eco-friendly on the negative it means disgust.

Gold

Positive: divinity, Godhead, righteousness, nature of God (1 Cor. 3:12-13, Exo. 25:10-11, 17, Hag. 2:8), or faith (1 Pet. 1:7).

Negative: greed, a counterfeit of God's nature.

Silver

Positive: redemption, *"Silver (Exo. 30:13; Lev. 27:3) is redemption money (Lev. 17:10-11: 1 Pet 1:18, 1 Cor. 6:20:3). Silver in the Old Testament is equivalent to blood, it is the blood money used for redemption (ransom money paid to God). It was this silver that was brought together to make the foundation of the Tabernacle. ... Thus, everything in the entire Tabernacle sat on silver sockets. ...the entire structure rests upon the blood of Jesus Christ."* Dr. Chuck Missler Exodus Notes pg.124.

Negative: the Bible Hebrew word for silver is *keseph* the same word used for money, hence its primitive root means to fear, be greedy, and have a desire, long, sore.

Cream White

That which concerns finances, financial prosperity.

Precious Stones and Colors

N.B In the Old Testament there were precious stones found on the breastplate of the High Priest ephod (High Priest garment). They were placed on its chest as God had commanded; they were to constantly stand as a reminder in the Presence of God, of His chosen people.

> *"Make the breastplate for decision-making as creatively as you make the ephod. Make it out of gold, violet, purple, and bright red yarn and out of fine linen yarn. Fold it in half so that it's 9 inches square. Fasten four rows of precious stones on it. In the first row put red quartz, topaz, and emerald. In the second row put turquoise, sapphire, and crystal. In the third row put jacinth, agate, and amethyst. In the fourth row put beryl, onyx, and gray quartz. Mount them in gold settings. The stones correspond to the 12 sons of Israel, by name, each stone engraved (like a signet*

ring) with the name of one of the 12 tribes." Exo. 28:15-21 GW.

Now I will go into details about the meaning of these stones starting from the firstborn Reuben to the last, Benjamin.

Sardis (Rosy red)

This gemstone was to represent the tribe of Reuben in color it is rosy red in representing the Redemption which is by Jesus Christ. The name Reuben means, 'here is my Son.' This implies God providing His only begotten Son as a sacrifice (Joh 3:16).

Topaz (tan brown)

The gem stone's color is tan brown, the color represents what is earthly, a type of Jesus coming in the flesh to be our Mediator before God as the name Simeon means 'Hearing,' connoting the idea of Him interceding for us before God His Father.

Carbuncle (blood red)

Its color is blood red, representing Jesus' work of atonement and purchasing us with His own life on the cross, this is the tribe from which comes the Priesthood, Levi.

Emerald

Its color is brilliant green representing provision and prosperity (grass-like color), a type of Jesus as our provider and caretaker in the form of a Shepherd, the name of the tribe represented here is Judah meaning 'Praise,' from which Jesus emanates.

Sapphire (royal blue)

Its color is royal blue representing the Kingly office of Jesus, a form of power and authority, the tribe represented here is Dan meaning, 'He judges,' both judging those who are lost and the defeater of the devil for us.

Diamond

The color here is brilliantly clear, a type of Christ's sufferings and coming out victorious that in Him we should not suffer, as the name for this tribe is Naphtali meaning, 'My struggle.'

Ligure/Jacinth (dark deep blue)

The color is dark deep blue, representing favor, the name for this tribe is Gad meaning, 'I'm lucky (fortunate),' a type of Christ bringing us privileges and special rights.

Agate/Cameo (Orange)

Its color is orange, a type of Christ bringing us blessings, the name of this tribe is Asher meaning, 'Blessing.'

Amethyst (purple)

The color of this gemstone is purple, a type of Christ as one with full dominion and highest position, the tribe represented here is Issachar meaning, 'Reward,' which is the gift of Salvation through all who have faith in Him.

Aquamarine/Beryl (turquoise)

The color here is turquoise, a type of Christ as our greatness, the tribe represented here is Zebulon meaning, 'Honor.'

Onyx (flesh pink)

Its color is flesh pink, a type of Christ-loving, representing His work as revealing the true nature of the Father, the tribe here is Joseph meaning, 'May He give Another.'

Jasper (transparent)

This last gem stone's color is transparency, a type of Christ as Faithful and True, the tribe represented here is Benjamin meaning, 'Son of My Right Hand,' which also gives us the last position and responsibility Jesus had to take of seating at His Father's Right Hand in Heaven to represent us.

Ruby (Deep red)

Wisdom (Job 28: 18 KJV, *"...for the price of wisdom is above rubies."*).

Pearl

Pearls come from an oyster. When an oyster is injured it secrets a certain hormone that mingles with the sand of the sea by such means pearls grow by accretion, they are removed from their place of growth to become an item of adornment. The oyster turns its pain and wound into a precious and one of the world's valuable stones, this is a picture of Christ on the cross turning defeat into victory, trials into triumphs. Pearls, therefore, imply victory, conquering, and triumph. Jews regarded the pearls as not kosher (unclean). The Lord Jesus comparing the Kingdom to a merchant seeking goodly pearl in Matthew 13: 45-46 must have not been appealing to His Jewish audience. The Lord understood that Jews only see the value of pearls because they sell them to gentiles. The sea in this context refers to the world, the merchant to Christ, and the pearls to the gentile believers. People who were once unclean and cast away from the commonwealth of Israel but are now engrafted in.

Bdellium

Bdellium is a pearl see the explanation above. Pearls are precious stones that represent the work of the Holy Spirit. They are forged through under earth pressure or by fire and are cut, meaning persecutions, trials, or tests that bring patience out of a believer.

Hearing God's voice in Dreams

Clothes

Clothes in dreams reveal our work of faith, what we are currently doing given our God-given assignment or seasonal purpose. They also reveal the position we have assumed before God as well as our condition before Him. Isa. 61:10 GW, *"I will find joy in the LORD. I will delight in my God. He has dressed me in the clothes of salvation. He has wrapped me in the robe of righteousness like a bridegroom with a priest's turban, like a bride with her jewels."*

When explaining clothes we will look into God's design and intent of the priestly garments:

"Then bring Aaron and his sons to the entrance of the tent of meeting, and wash them. Take the clothes, and put them on Aaron-the linen robe, the ephod and the robe that is worn with it, and the breastplate. Use the belt to tie it on him tightly. Put his turban on him, and fasten the holy crown to it. Take the anointing oil, pour it on his head, and anoint him. "Have his sons come forward. Dress them in their linen robes, and put turbans on them. Tie belts around the waists of Aaron and his sons. They alone are to be priests; this is a permanent law. In this way, you will ordain Aaron and his sons. Exo. 29:5-9 GW.

Apart from the priestly garments being an adornment of beauty and glory, they represented the perfect condition God willed to see His people. They were designed to exhibit righteousness and holiness, attributes of God's nature. Therefore the Holy Spirit chooses to speak to us concerning our work of purpose and of faith by what we wear. *"Clearly, all of you who were baptized in Christ's name have clothed yourselves with Christ."* Gal. 3:27 GW.

N.B I consider the definitions below from a positive standpoint of view. I do not cover the negative side, which would be based on the dream context, example dreaming yourself wearing a jersey in summer would mean being ready for a task whose season has already passed or worried about God's provision of comfort and supply in the face of a fruitful season. Always stay mindful of colors when seeking to understand the meaning of the clothes you were wearing in your dream.

Nakedness in dreams

Throughout the Bible, nakedness revealed humiliation and dishonor. Being clothed in Scriptures speaks of being covered, glorified, and honored. Remember in Genesis man was created naked and walked naked in the presence of God but after the fall man's nakedness became shame in the presence.

Hat

Your attitude (Job 29:14 CEV, *"Kindness and justice were my coat and hat."*). Your matters of submission under a local ministry, pastor, church leader, or to the Lord.

Cap

A promise of God's protection during a season of drought (the cap is worn during heat times, heat biblically conveys a drought or dry season*"The LORD is your guardian... The sun will not beat down on you during the day."* Psa. 121:5-6 GW. It also connotes flame meaning times of danger). Your current spiritual rank, like color, plays a significant role in this also.

Belt

Jesus in Revelation chapter 1 wore a gold belt around His waist. The waist is the point of connection between the upper body and the lower body, it is thus the balance of the whole body, meaning, Jesus is centered in Righteousness and Truth. A belt can signify the central point of your life, your spiritual foundations, honesty, truth, faithfulness, or either dishonesty, unfaithfulness, etc.

Short sleeve shirt

An unfinished formal task, i.e. work of ministry, job-related or business work (In the first chapter of the book of Revelation 'One like the Son of man' who appears to John is attributed to the one who appeared to Daniel in the tenth chapter. This is not Jesus so goes the simile One 'like' the Son of man, see Rev. 22:16. This messenger may be the same messenger that was sent to Daniel. In both instances, he is mentioned with seven attributes. One particular attribute that stands out is that in Daniel both his arms and legs are like polished bronze (Vs. 6) while in Revelation only his feet are mentioned as a fine bronze burning in a furnace. Vs 15. Recall that both books notably infer this messenger as wearing a robe, a linen clothing worn by the priests. In Daniel, the robe is short-sleeved while in Revelation we don't see the arms implying that the robe is long-sleeved. In Daniel it is short-sleeved because Christ's priesthood work is not yet fulfilled but in Revelation, it is long-sleeved to imply that Christ has fulfilled His priesthood roles in His redemptive work) or being half prepared, ready but not all prepared.

Long Sleeve Shirt

A finished formal task, (refer to the above explanation of the short sleeve shirt) or being prepared, being ready and prepared).

T-Shirt

An unfinished casual task, i.e. home, household, community, societal work (you normally wear t-shirts at home, not at work or when going to malls, etc.).

Underwear

Secrets, private things.

Vest

Secrecy, hidden things of the heart, hidden motives

Ladies tights

Personal beliefs, hidden thoughts, and motives concerning your journey and walk.

Formal pants

That which concerns your formal current or future journey can be in ministry, business, or work. This can also mean your service.

Suit

Ministry of occupation work or business work.

Coat

Justice (righteousness) and kindness (judgment), (Job 29:14 CEV, *"Kindness and justice were my coat and hat."*), spirit of influence and leadership (Isa. 3:6 GW, *"A person will grab one of his relatives from his father's family and say, "You have a coat. You'll be our leader. This pile of ruins will be under your control."*).

Casual pants (i.e. jeans)

Not taking your vacation or work seriously or being relaxed/casual about your journey.

Vintage wear

Being called for a classic type of ministry, a long-standing type of ministry, traditionally styled ministry, having a responsibility to carry on a long-standing tradition.

Scotch cloth

To stop something from happening, to thwart.

Leather

To hide, be hidden, conceal, secrete.

Shorts

Not prepared or still unfit for the coming or already at hand task.

Jacket

Protection from spiritual seasons and situations that are not favorable. Your emotional feelings.

Jersey

Being comforted and cared for by God, nurtured or catered for during a stressful or uncomforting season of your life or your welcoming of something, zealous and accepting of the expected task or role.

Skirt

A task or journey that demands a thorough preparation such as changing or preparing yourself in heart and wiring yourself mentally before invoking yourself in it (you cannot wear a skirt alone without a top, a skirt is an item of clothing that demands females to wear it with a top).

Dress

A task or journey you have been prepared for that requires less or no preparation on your side to invoke init (a dress is not like a skirt it needs no top since a dress is a clothing design that is one fabric from top to bottom).

Short/mini skirt

Exposed to people that you are not prepared and ready for the task at hand (a short skirt is revealing to the thighs).

Apron

A task that calls for you to serve or to wait on people.

Tie

Your level of seriousness, commitment, reverence, or devotion.

School uniform

In a positive sense, it means having a teachable spirit, an attitude to learn, and having humility. Dreaming of wearing a school uniform in a negative sense means not willing to outgrow a certain mistake, experience, or mental attitude. It also means you are not learning the lesson God would have you learn out of a particular situation.

Work uniform

Mentally and emotively ready, which is being prepared and ready for the given task.

Workout clothes

In a process of being prepared by God and readied for the coming task or work.

Sports clothes

A preparation process that might not be taken seriously because of seeming fun and playful.

Wedding gown

A wake-up call for you to review your commitment, devotion, and surrender toward the Lord.

Veil

That which concerns your flesh, covering, blindness, looking to the end of that which is passing away, the law.

Traditional clothes

This concerns people of your culture, your nation, your God-given responsibility for your locals or a particular people or culture. In the negative sense, it means you are bogged down by your traditional beliefs you hold concerning God or you're calling you therefore need to rewire your belief system.

Wearing a wedding theme attire

This represents you have put on your attitude, readied, and prepared for the Kingdom (specifically God's will for your life on earth). Mat. 22:11 GW, *"When the king came to see the guests, he saw a person who was not dressed in the wedding clothes provided for the guests."*

Linen

It speaks of righteousness. On the negative side, it speaks of man's work, man's righteousness, Isa. 64:6b GW, *"...and all our righteous acts are like permanently stained rags."* The linen is made up of a thread or cloth made of flax, a flax is a plant, a plant that comes from the ground that which is cursed, and also meaning man's efforts that are cursed. God forbade Israel from wearing a garment made of both wool and linen (Deu. 22:11), it's because linen represented man's righteousness while wool represented God's kind of righteousness, see wool below.

Wool

Dreaming of someone wearing wool clothes means they are true followers of Christ, on the other hand, Jesus in Matthew 7 verse 15 spoke of wolves dressed in sheep clothing (wool) this means they visibly appear as wolves though they hide under the wool (false prophets, false followers of Christ). If you dream of putting on wool clothing it means God's need for you to put on the attitude and character of a disciple (sheep). Wool was obtained by the shedding of a sheep's blood (Christ's righteousness).

Shoes

Shoes have to do with where God is taking you and a given mission or assignment, Eph. 6:15 GW, *"Put on your shoes so that you are ready to spread the Good News that gives peace."*

Barefoot

In a negative context, unwillingness, unpreparedness to do a particular mission or assignment. To be barefoot in a dream also implies unexpected suffering on the journey ahead please refer to the Foreword concerning a dream I related. In a positive context, it refers to your humility or entering into God's rest, Exo. 3:5, *"God said, "Don't come any closer! Take off your sandals because this place where you are standing is holy ground."* GW.

Shoes without socks

Taking on a mission or work that makes you feel uncomfortable. It might also mean doing something that you are not well adjusted for.

Formal shoes

Currently or about to undertake a formal assignment and also prepared.

Heels

God is escalating you to an assignment higher than the one you had or a higher spiritual position than the current one.

Women's flat shoes

Being required to carry on with your common or usual ministry or walk in the Lord, a simple or regular ministry or walk. On the negative, it means a dull, boring, or uninteresting walk or journey.

Running shoes

In a positive context, it reveals God bringing you to an amusing journey or assignment and you're being required to speed up things. In a negative dream context, it reveals your playful attitude toward a specific mission or assignment.

Sandals

In a positive context, it reveals an assignment that does not require you to be serious, a casual mission. In a negative context, it reveals your unpreparedness and you're not serious concerning your current mission.

Slippers

God requiring you to put on an attitude of rest (slippers are shoes worn indoors and in the bedroom).

Boots

A task that will be testing and will require tenacity and perseverance.

Big/unfitting shoes

Stepping outside of the boundaries of your calling to doing something you are not called for, an assignment that isn't yours or being ahead of yourself, moving too fast to fulfill assigned duties which require you to mature first, presently trying to fulfill what is meant to be done in the later stage.

Hearing God's voice in Dreams

The Ministry Gifts in Colors

The fivefold or call it ministry gifts, the Apostle, Prophet, Evangelist, Pastor, and Teacher, see Eph. 4:11 and refer to fingers on the section of this book titled *Body Parts in dreams*. Each of these offices can be represented by colors also in dreams. If you dream of wearing a t-shirt, since a t-shirt represents an assignment that is not yet completed with the following colors it speaks of your calling being in one of these ministry offices below:

Many colors t-shirt

Called to stand in the office of an apostle (the apostolic office is the only office that functions in all the offices. Apostles can be prophets, evangelists, pastors, or teachers depending on the Holy Spirit as He sees a need. This means when you put all the colors together which represent all the ministries they make up the color black. It has to be only a black t-shirt, not the whole attire and the context of the dream has to be positive or when you interpret the black t-shirt search for peace in your heart it will direct you to the right meaning).

Blue t-shirt

Called to function in the office of a prophet (blue is the color of revelation, prophets are called to operate in the revelation gifts refer to chapter 6 *Difference between Dreams and visions*).

Red t-shirt

Called to operate in the office of an evangelist (the color red represents salvation, the heralds of salvation are evangelists).

Brown t-shirt

Called to operate in the pastoral office (the color brown represents nurturing which is a character of shepherds. In the New

Testament Greek the word for shepherd is the same word for the pastor).

White t-shirt

Called to operate in the teaching office (the color white represents clarity, teachers in the church are called to clarify the Word of God).

Actions in Dreams

Walking

This has to do with your destiny, where you are going in the future, your current walk of faith or walk of purpose.

Running

This reveals spiritual warfare, or your running away from that which the Lord requires you to do, avoiding the Lord's calling. It also means hastening to finish or to do something or a particular project.

Waken from sleep

Dreaming waken from sleep means something will catch you by surprise.

Eating

Eating in dreams means being taken care of as a child of God. Since we are in Africa I will do justice to explain this notion as many people have gotten into trouble eating in dreams which can be dangerous, again the context of the dream is important. Is the dream of a negative or positive context? You have to be very careful not to be so worried about this as the Lord has already taken care of us as believers in this area, Mar 16:17-18 GW, *"These are the miraculous signs that will accompany believers: They will use the power and authority of my name to force demons out of people. They will speak new languages. They will pick up snakes, and if they drink any deadly poison, it will not hurt them. They will place their hands on the sick and cure them."* If the dream was negative as many people have been poisoned through dreams, in Africa such experiences are common, do not concern yourself with having eaten in a dream but rather concern yourself with the fact that you did finish the food, If you finished the meal in the dream you might immediately resort to prayer but if you did not finish the meal this means you conquered against the evil plot.

Eating bread

It means eating the Word of God. In the Old Testament was a meal-offering, it was offered to God through the priest. The offerer of this type of offering was required to eat from it, this meal represented fellowship between Jehovah and man, eating therefore in the Bible is the highest order of fellowship.

Eating strong meat

Eating strong meat in the dream means eating matured stuff of the Word of God, see Heb. 5:14.

Receiving a cake

An upcoming event of celebration, joy, and gladness to your life. Eating a cake in a positive context means about to experience a happy moment or about to participate in a celebration event or jubilant experience. In a negative context eating a cake means to be wounded (demonically inflicted with sickness) or to profane or defile yourself from the Hebrew cake root word *chalal*. If it's your birthday cake in a dream it means a spiritual or a real-life promotion, you are about to jubilantly grow in a certain area of your life. Given a wedding cake means a potential surprise for marriage if you are a woman if you are a single man it means about to meet your soul mate.

Receiving a present

In a positive meaning, it means about to be surprised by something good. In a negative meaning, it means something that will negatively surprise you.

Drinking milk

This means you are either obligated to eat from the elementary teachings of the Word of God if you are sucking milk from a bottle it means you need to outgrow the elementary teachings of the Word to matured stuff.

Rain wet

If you dream wet of a spring or summer rain it means blessings or overflow but if the dream was of heavy rainfall it means dishonor or shame.

Sleeping

Unaware, ignorant, not wary, or oblivious to situations or a specific situation around your life.

Urinating

Being relieved or being given the ability to take care of business.

Resting

Responding in faith and trust upon God concerning what you are going through or a given situation you are facing, at ease, calm, and having confidence in God.

Flying

Operating in the spirit or by faith, being carefree, above problems and situations, God taking you to a higher level concerning the things of the spirit it may be a prophetic gifting or more grace in the realm of visions and revelations.

Fighting

Many times this reveals spiritual warfare, to be involved or about to be engaged in an argument, conflict, or misunderstanding with someone.

Driving

To be in charge, to lead a ministry (it can be a pastoral, prophetic, intercessory, home cell ministry, a prayer group, or particular people).

Cooking

Serving or waiting on people.

Cleaning/Bathing

Putting away stuff that is unnecessary in your life, purifying, a process of sanctification.

Worshipping

This might mean a calling to be involved in the ministry of worship, called to praise, a call to prophesy, gifts of utterance (divers kinds of tongues, interpretation of tongues or the gift of prophecy), to lead worshippers (believers).

Playing

Lacking seriousness concerning godly things, not giving necessary attention to spiritual matters, the need to pursue spiritual maturity. Orgy, sexual sins (Exo. 32:6 KJV, *and the people sat down to eat and to drink, and rose up to play*.).

Laughing

The joy of the spirit, a tone of victory concerning something you felt worried about or something you have been praying for, worrying less, not anxious.

Crying

A season of heartache and tests coming ahead or something that will be touching enough to make you cry.

Watching

The Lord is revealing a vision to you it might concern you personally, it may be someone you know or something you are acquainted with.

Kissing

Fond of someone, affection, engagement, covenant, a deep and personal relationship, commitment, and an agreement.

Sex

This is one aspect of dreams you need to be careful of, it can be tricky. 1Co 10:8 KJV, *"Neither let us commit fornication, as some of them committed, and fell in one day three and twenty thousand."* The meaning of the word fornication in the preceding verse goes a long way than just sexual sins or sex before marriage as in dreams also. In the context of the preceding verse it expresses the sin of the worship of Ashtoreth and Molech which the children of Israel committed against God and as well as sexual sins committed with the daughters of Moab that same day, see Num. 25:1-6, 9. In dreams also when you dream of sleeping with someone it can mean idolizing something that seeks to take the place of God in your life, it can be your girlfriend, boyfriend, money, success, fame, etc.

Apart from the above explanation, there is yet another danger to dreaming of sexual sins, this applies to a male who constantly wakes up with wet dreams and a female who wakes up wet too from such dreams. In this case, it was not just a dream but it might mean deeper than that. This might imply the lusts of the flesh that the individual is entertaining in their thought pattern, they grow to a point of soulish dreams. This can be so dangerous that it can attract spirits of oppression. Some people have carried this burden to marriages, many a times relationships and marriages under this attack crumble. Many are prone to never enjoy marital sex due to this oppression. It can help you to see your pastor as a male, a woman leader in the church, or pastor's wife for a woman or you can rather stand on the Word of God, daily Scripture studying to transform your mind and daily Scripture confessions against this as the Holy Spirit will set you free.

Cheating

It means spiritual unfaithfulness, giving something else other than the Lord priority over your life (see Sex above), violating God's rules for your advantage, dishonest dealings, trickery.

Falling

Something that will cause you to draw back in the faith, a setback, or something that will be humiliating. This falls under warning dreams, it calls for you to pray.

Drunkenness

Being under influence, it can be people or demonic influence.

Reading

A call to apply diligence to your study of the Word, a certain area of your life you are called to do an introspection of, devotion and commitment to your calling and purpose.

Writing an exam

In a positive sense, it means a life test. In the negative sense it means exposing an area of attack to the enemy, the context of the dream will reveal this, many times in such dreams the Lord will protect you, you might wake up not having written anything on your exam paper.

Taking a selfie pic

A need to look into yourself, a need for a self-inventory. On the negative, it means self-idolizing, self-centeredness, self-glorification, and self-exaltation.

Being taken a picture

It also means to surmount, to overcome, and to be praised, elevated.

Taking a picture with someone

It means sharing an experience with that person or someone.

Writing

The requirement for you to plan purposefully concerning your destiny or a certain mission, laying out your future, the need for you to prophesy over your future.

Planting

The need to sow the Word into your mind and spirit or to sow finances to a specific person or ministry, to sow service to someone or something.

Harvesting

Either God is revealing to you that you are in a season of harvesting everything you have sown before or He drawing your attention to expect a harvest, evangelism, soul-winning.

Training

Preparing or being prepared for a given task.

Learning

You are required to be teachable, diligently learn, or to observe a specific instruction or lesson.

Swimming

Flowing in the Spirit (Holy Spirit), involved in a personal move of the Spirit, inspiration.

Going backward

Regressing in the things of faith.

Shaking a hand

About to meet someone, closing a deal, about to come into an agreement

Signing

Authorizing or something you have authorized in the spirit, consenting to defeat or victory through your words (confession), a deal.

Buying

Accessing things through your faith, claiming what belongs to you.

Selling

To exchange, to offer something, swap or forfeiting spiritual virtues or gifts, despising the gift(s) of God, profane, fornication (Gen. 25:33, Heb. 12:16).

Giving an offering

Dreaming of giving an offering in the church reveals your degree of surrendering depending on the amount you give.

Playing sport

It means to delight yourself (Isa. 57:4). It also means mischief (Prov. 10:23, 26:19), to play, laugh, mock, disdain (Jdg. 16:25 & 27).

Playing soccer

Facing a group of opponents and you being required to work in a team. Usually, such dreams occur when your church, where your fellowship is facing a tight opposition from the community or it may concern a formidable competition in business. Such dreams may come as playing rugby, American football, hockey, etc. If you are losing it reveals being at a disadvantage and if winning it reveals victory.

Playing tennis

Facing a single opponent that opposes your labor can be at work, in business, or ministry.

Playing chess

Facing a single opponent that opposes your ideas, intellectual capacity, emotionally trying to strain you and close in on your moves.

Playing cards

An amusing experience, using a resource to achieve a purpose or about to be involved in an argument that is set to achieve a purpose.

People in Dreams

In this aspect, your relationship with the participant in the dream is important i.e. a brother, sister, or your spouse. Below we will explain what it means when you see the following characters in dreams.

N.B we are focusing on dreams that reveal a key role played by the following characters in a particular dream. Do not confuse your dreaming **about** your brother, your spouse, sister, etc. When the dream is **about** any of the following characters then the character is referred to, for example, if you dream **about** your spouse or sister, brother, etc. then the message is directly intended to that person.

Father

When you dream of your father or a certain father this is to reveal the character of God in view of His will, intents, purposes, and plans concerning your life. In layman's terms, the Lord might be concerned about you doing or fulfilling His will. God as a source and more specific His aspect of Love as a Father, 2 Cor. 13: 14 and many other New Testament verses attribute the nature of love to God.

Woman/Mother

The New Jerusalem from above (Gal. 4:26), the nation of Israel (Rev. 12:1-2), a system of worship, idolatry and harlotry (Rev. 17:5), religion.

Brother

The manifestation of the Lord Jesus in a dream as your brother, Col 1:18 GW, *"He is also the head of the church, which is his body. He is the beginning, the first to come back to life so that he would have first place in everything."* He reveals Himself in this manner to connote you're being a joint heir with Him, His protection and personal affiliation with you. Such a dream concerns matters of your inheritance and possessing of promises in the Kingdom. Depending on the context of the dream, for example, you are going through something with a certain brother who you fellowship with, this has nothing to do with the Lord Jesus but it's a message you are given through a dream that concerns that particular brother and you.

Sister

It is either a message that is directed or includes a certain female believer in your place of fellowship depending on the context of the dream it also means nurturing, care, and love. A sister also means wisdom (Prov. 7:4a GW, *"Say to wisdom, "You are my sister."*).

A female relative

Support structure or wisdom (Prov. 7:4b KJV, *"and call understanding thy kinswoman."*).

Beautiful female caretaker

Divine favor, or angelic succoring.

Female child

Your gift (personal gift), calling (your work), grace, blessing, and benevolence that is still immature not yet developed or it can mean your desire, that which you desire dearly. (Do not confuse with a male child (which is a ministry)).

Male child

Your God-given ministry (people you are set to lead, church, prayer group, etc.), your calling, assignment, that which you have been entrusted with and has not yet grown.

Children

The promising rewards, partially grown but not fully matured rewards or fruits of your labor or work. They can also mean your blessings or heritage in the Kingdom of God.

Woman

A woman in Scriptures means the Holy Spirit like the woman in Jesus' parables who lost and searched till she found her coin, which is a figure of the Holy Spirit searching in the world and finding the missing (sinners), see Lk. 15:8-10 or the parable of the woman who hid leaven in three measures of meal which is the Holy Spirit allowing false prophets and teachers into the Church to reveal the genuine believers from the counterfeit, see Mat. 13:33.

His manifestation as a woman in a dream is to reveal His personality of communion, sensitivity, nurturing, and care throughout the New Testament He is revealed as the God of fellowship, 2 Cor. 13:14. At times this might be revealing His longing for your fellowship and communion.

Grandfather

An old system of leadership, overused, or a mentor, a spiritual leader with seasoned experience.

Old man

Experience, wisdom (Job 32:7 GW, *"I thought, 'Age should speak, and experience should teach wisdom."*).

Grandmother

Old teaching, ideology, tradition, philosophy that might be running in your place of fellowship, family, community, or workplace.

Next of kin

A dream manifestation of Jesus Christ as your redeemer, *"The primary meaning of the Hebrew. go'el is 'one who enforces a* claim' which has lapsed; so 'one who re-claims' or 're-vindicates.' Hence the verb is used of redeeming a house or field after it has been sold, or an Israelite who has been obliged to sell himself as a slave." –Cambridge Bible for Schools and Colleges. In a dream where you see a kinsman-redeemer be assured of restoration, defense, and victory over your enemies as one of the *goel's* (kinsman redeemer's) responsibility involved avenging of blood, see Deu. 19:6 & 12.

Bride

The Body of Christ, the Church of Jesus Christ, in the New Testament the Church is recognized as a chastise virgin (2 Cor. 11:2, Mat. 25:1-13). She is not yet a wife, the marriage is futuristic it will take place during the rapture (Rev. 19:7).

Groom

A dream manifestation of Christ as committed to you, as well as being your provider, supplier, caretaker, and lover.

Husband

A dream manifestation of Christ as your Lord assuming all the responsibilities of your life and this is given His demand for your total submission to Him.

Wife

Your ministry, the people you are called to serve, as a wife depends on her husband emotionally and in satisfaction of her physical needs so do the people you are called to serve.

Baby

A gift, (see male and female child above).

Boyfriend/girlfriend

Familiarity.

Ex-boyfriend/ex-girlfriend

Former experience

Friend

The close companionship of the Holy Spirit in your times of need and helplessness, Pro 18:24 ESV, *"A man of many companions may come to ruin, but there is a friend who sticks closer than a brother."*

Neighbor

Any individual that needs your help, this includes the people around your life, see Lk. 10:30-27.

Guest

This is an angelic being in your dream, Heb. 13:2 GW, *"Don't forget to show hospitality to believers you don't know. By doing this some believers have shown hospitality to angels without being aware of it."*

Wedding guest

A wedding guest represents one invited to the Kingdom of God (Matt. 22: 2-3a GW, *"The kingdom of heaven is like a king who planned a wedding for his son. He sent his servants to those who had been invited to the wedding).*

Friendly giant

An angelic being in your dream that shows itself strongly on your behalf in terms of protection and safety. If you are walking with him it infers being secured on the troubles of the journey ahead. A giant in a dream can also mean a person of great faith in the negative it can be a formidable force in the spirit realm.

Faceless person

Many times in the Old Testament a faceless person is a type of the Holy Spirit. In the book of redemption, the book of Ruth, Naomi is a type of Israel, Ruth is a type of the Church and Boaz is the type of Christ. Rth. 2:5-6 GW, *"Then said Boaz unto his servant that was set over the reapers, whose damsel is this? And the servant that was set over the reapers answered and said, it is the Moabitish damsel that came back with Naomi out of the country of Moab."* Notice, the introducer of Ruth to Boaz is the faceless servant, the introducer of the Church to Christ is the Holy Spirit. Also, see Genesis 37:15-17. A faceless person in your dream can also mean an angel.

Pastor's wife

The local ministry where you are submitting, your role or matters concerning your submission to your local church. If you dream your pastor's wife placing a demand on you it means the Holy Spirit is revealing to you a certain gap in your local ministry that only you can fill.

Employee/Boss

The manifestation of the Lord Jesus in your dream concerning your stewardship, Lk 12:42 Webster, *"And the Lord said, who then is that faithful and wise steward, whom his lord shall make ruler over his household, to give them their portion of provisions in due season?"*

King

The manifestation of the lordship and kingship of Christ in your dream, Rev 19:16 CEV, *On the part of the robe that covered his thigh was written, "KING OF KINGS AND LORD OF LORDS."* By this, He is drawing your attention to your loyalty and service to Him.

Judge

If you see yourself as a judge in a dream the Lord is awakening you to a need to not compromise but to speak out to a particular person or groups concerning the person's or groups' inconsistencies to the Word of God, see 1 Pet. 4:17. This can also mean the Lord revealing to you a specified area or an issue that needs to be corrected, this specifically deals with issues of holiness in violation of His Word according to as the dream will reveal. In a negative context, it points to the devil condemning you the word Satan means prosecutor at law (sometimes dreaming a prosecuting attorney), see Rom. 8:1. Every time you are accused by your thoughts that is the enemy, the devil is the fault finder God is the solution finder. God only corrects, rebukes, and exhorts but does not condemn.

Queen

Women in God's Kingdom are not queens but kings. A city that is a cult stronghold, a woman who is a ruler in the kingdom of darkness over a city or community, see Eph. 6:12.

Rich man

An individual able to minister to the needs of another or the manifestation of Christ as able to meet your needs and wants. In the negative context, it means greed (Mat. 19:24).

Nobleman

The word is also translated as prince in other New Testament versions of the Bible, this is a manifestation of Christ as appointed by the Father over His Kingdom, see Lk. 19:12-27. On the opposite side the devil is also referred to as the prince of this world, see Joh. 12:31 and 2 Cor. 4:4. The fallen angels are also called the princes of this world, 1Co 2:8 KJV, *"Which none of the princes of this world knew: for had they known it, they would not have crucified the Lord of glory."* The preceding verse does not talk about the government that crucified Christ but the spirits behind them.

Male President

Dreaming of a male president is a manifestation of the Lord as the head of God's administration system, representative of God and the embodiment of His rule and carrying out His will. Any message of a male president in a dream is a direct message from the Lord Jesus.

Female President

This means the governor of the Kingdom of God on earth the Person of the Holy Spirit (see Woman, above). He is the only Person of the Godhead that is present with the Church on earth. Any message from a female president in a dream is a direct message from the Person of the Holy Spirit.

Government official

This includes those called to operate in church leadership, Paul refers to it as governments, 1 Cor. 12:28. The Kingdom of God's system of hierarchy and administration, reveals the Kingdom's decision on something that concerns you. In the negative context, it speaks of agents or certain spirits in control in the kingdom of darkness.

School principal

Someone called to pastor churches, an apostolic office, or the manifestation of Christ as the ultimate Apostle or overseer, see Heb. 3:1. In a negative sense, it reveals demonic spirits that rule over the lowest spirits known as the powers, see Eph. 6:12 or refer to my book The Prophecy.

Schoolteacher

In the teaching ministry or office, someone called to teach. If the school teacher is you in the dream this means the Lord is calling you to teach His Word. This may also mean a process of being taught by the Holy Spirit on a particular lesson or subject of Scripture.

Security guard

Your need to protect something or for you to defend the faith, Jud. 3. It also alludes to God's angelic system of security and protection.

Bodyguard

In chapter 7 we touched on the subject of angels differing in service and departments. Security guards also refer to guardian angels who are set charge over your life, see Psa. 91:11.

Thief

The devil, Joh 10:10 GW, *"A thief comes to **steal**, kill, and destroy. But I came so that my sheep will have life and so that they will have everything they need."*

Harlot

False devotion, false worship (religion), false doctrine (belief), feign love, flatteries.

Soldiers

God's angelic system of warfare and defense, the Message Translation of the Bible in place of God of Hosts calls Him the God of the Angel Armies.

Police

Being called to bring order in the Body of Christ, is one of the gifts Paul calls ministry, see Rom. 12:7. This can also mean God's system of extraterrestrial force for enforcing the divine laws and granted the authority to keep human affairs in order. When you dream of police chasing you this means a certain heavenly sanction has been ruled against you based on your having not complied or because of breaking a particular divine law.

Traffic officer

This means you are to assume a pastoral responsibility or to correct and exhort. Also means God's system of intervention for inspecting and dictating compliance concerning our obedience and submission to His instruction concerning our purpose fulfillment. When you dream of being stopped or pulled up by a traffic officer it is time for you to review your walk and submission according to the divine instruction and laws of the road given.

Seller/shop owner

This means the Person of the Holy Spirit as the giver of graces and gifts according to as God dictates according to His will for each of us. Dreaming yourself as a seller means you are called to teach and speak to people's lives that you make them discover their destinies. When dreaming of owning a shop it means you are called to discover and equip leaders.

Doctor

This means Christ's manifestation to you as a healer either of your emotional or physical inadequacies. It can also specifically point out His sufficient strength for you when struggling to rid yourself of a particular sin. In this aspect, He is pointing you to His grace and power that is able to help you when your self-efforts fail. Dreaming yourself as a doctor means you are called into the ministry of divine healing, laying hands on the sick.

Nurse

Ministry for the old age, a ministry for the broken and the hurting, caretaker, compassion.

Shoemaker

This points to the work of the Holy Spirit as a restorer of destinies, assignments, and a rewriter of failures along with our earthly frailties. Seeing yourself as a shoemaker means being called to counsel, advise, teach, or pastor people.

Waiter

The ministry of angels as your servants in the Kingdom, Heb. 1:14 KJV, *"Are they not all ministering spirits, sent forth to minister for them who shall be heirs of salvation?"* The salvation alluded to here is the Greek *Soteria* Strong defines it, *"as a (properly abstract) noun; rescue or safety (physically or morally): - deliver, health, salvation, save, saving."* The word connotes a package of healing, prosperity, deliverance, rescue, and wealth. You might get such a dream when you have been praying on something that has already been provided for and God is calling your attention to this service of angels, your need to command them in Jesus' Name because God has already done everything He could about your situation. You only need to personally command things to manifestation etc. If you are the waiter or waitress in the dream it means your call to serve, waiting on people or it reminds you that your calling or gift is meant to serve others.

Shepherd

In a time of need the Lord may choose to reveal Himself as your shepherd in a dream, this means He is your caretaker and your provider that leads you by the quiet waters. A dream like this is also likely to appear when you feel you need the Lord's guidance on a straining situation that demands a well thought out decision. If you dream of yourself as a shepherd this means your call to pastor people, to assume ministerial leadership responsibility.

Treasure finder

The saving work of the Lord, His manifestation as a treasure finder, when He found us we were junk but He saw us as jewels, see Mat. 13: 44. This reveals how our Lord has beautiful eyes, eyes that see beyond our weaknesses and failures. If you dream of yourself as a treasure finder you are being called into evangelism, soul-winning.

Merchant

The ministry of the Lord in finding us broken and naked, how He found us and decked us with apparels of glory and rewards of opulence, He turned our sorrows into joy and mourning into songs of joy, see Mat. 13: 45-46. The Lord normally appears like this to reveal to you how He is able to turn your pain into health, Rom 8:28 GW, *"We know that all things work together for the good of those who love God-those whom he has called according to his plan."* When you see a merchant in your dream know that tables are about to turn in your favor. If you dream of yourself as a merchant know the Lord is giving you a responsibility to mend the broken, help the feeble, you can call it an intercessory grace.

Foreigner

This is a dream that reveals the presence of an extraterrestrial being around your life it can either be an angel of light or darkness depending on what you sensed or perceived in the dream. This can also be literal like about to be involved or called to people outside your borders.

Murderer

The devil, he is the ultimate and the first murderer, see Joh. 8:44 and *"A thief comes to steal, **kill**, and destroy. But I came so that my sheep will have life and so that they will have everything they need."*

Father in law

In the Hebrew, it comes from the word *Chomah,* which means to join, a wall of protection, walled, hedge, enclosure, defender. Dreaming of a father in law is seeing into a family situation, things that concern the intimations of marriage. In a negative context, it means a wall of partition, division, separation, or finding yourself in a place without protection.

Mother in law

That which concerns a marriage relationship, things that concern tenderness, affection, embrace. In a negative context, it may refer to issues of the hardness of heart, dislike, mistrust, and indifference.

Actor/Actress

Someone who plays a role that is not theirs.

Clown

To act or to be silly, buffoon, fool, or foolish.

Crazy person

A lunatic spirit (demonic spirits of madness and suicide).

A dead person

This is what the Bible calls a familiar spirit (Lev. 19:31, 20:6, Deu. 18:11, Isa. 8:19). There is a class of demons that fall under the demonic rank called powers, see Eph. 6:12. These demons closely observe families and individual lives that when they are dead they can easily mimic them in dreams. According to the Bible the dead *"know not anything ...neither have they any more forever a portion in all that is done under the sun."* Ecc. 9:5b-6 Darby. You get families that struggle in a specific area of life, it might be getting married, and divorce, premature death, stagnancy, etc. these are the demons responsible for that. When my mother passed away my grief led me to constantly dream of her, she would be serving me food or helping me with something. My mother died of a swollen heart. Shortly, after that, I experienced heart contractions because of my knowledge of Scriptures I began standing on the Word of God. If you dream of talking, hugging, kissing, walking, or eating food given by someone that has passed on it is the devil's trick to have you in agreement with a familiar spirit roaming around your family. Remember over 90% of our dreams are spiritual. The devil has no power or access over your life except you give him. On waking up command such a spirit to flee from you. If it was two dead people from your family that is two familiar spirits. Faith is specific you will need to name them like, *"You two familiar spirits revealed in my dream I command you to immediately stop with your plots, maneuvers, and operations against my life and my families' in Jesus' Name."* You only command once, commanding twice will open you prey to the enemy because you will be stepping outside of faith into unbelief.

Animals in Dreams

Lion

The Lord Jesus Christ (Rev 5:5 GW, *"Then one of the leaders said to me, "Stop crying! The Lion from the tribe of Judah, the Root of David, has won the victory. He can open the scroll and the seven seals on it."*), dominion, kingship, rulership, strength, strategy, and power. In a negative dream context, it means the enemy (1 Pet. 5:8 GW, *"Keep your mind clear, and be alert. Your opponent the devil is prowling around like a roaring lion as he looks for someone to devour."*).

Eagle

A prophetic calling or gift, the eagle is the king of the air this means being given a mantle to operate at a certain level in the realms of the spirit, being above situations also means rejuvenation, refreshed, renewed, and strengthened (Isa. 40:31), vision and great foresight.

Hawk

To glare, genius, be bright-colored, sparkle, to function within your sphere of calling (blossom), to glory. It also means flashing speed.

Birds

In a positive sense, it means being kept, cared for, and provided for (Mat. 6:26). In a negative sense, it means demons, devils (Mar. 4:4, Gen. 40:17-19).

Raven

Greed (a raven is the greediest bird) or darkness.

Owl

Hearing God's voice in Dreams

A night specter, owls are lovers of desolate and ruined places and the tombs, they also mean a demon.

Pelican

A haunting spirit, like an owl it is also a lover is of desolate and ruined places.

Vulture

Demonic or one who profits from the suffering of others.

Ostrich

In a positive sense, it means speed, hasten, fast (the ostrich runs faster than the fastest horse, see Job 39:18). In a negative sense it means foolishness, carelessness, unconcerned about your work and efforts (Job 39:13-17 GW, *"An ostrich proudly flaps her wings, but not because she loves her young. She abandons her eggs and lets the dusty ground keep them warm. And she doesn't seem to worry that the feet of an animal could crush them all. She treats her eggs as though they were not her own, unconcerned that her work might be for nothing. I made her foolish and without common sense."*).

Sheep

Believers, matured children of God, disciples, the followers of the Shepherd (Christ), they that can hear the voice of the Lord, (Joh. 10:4 GW, *"After he has brought out all his sheep, he walks ahead of them. The sheep follow him because they recognize his voice."*).

Goat

Sin, bully, rebellion (the second covering of the Tabernacle in the wilderness was of goat's skins, this was a type of Christ made sin with our sins on the cross). Goat(s) also means unbelievers, Mat. 25:33 & 41, GW, *"He will put the sheep on his right but the goats on his left. Then the king will say to those on his left, 'Get away from me! God has cursed you! Go into everlasting fire that was prepared for the devil and his angels!"*).

Cow/bull

Strength, leadership, carrying others burdens, power (a cow also represents one who has preeminence, to come first, it is represented by the Hebrew first letter *Aleph*. It also means chieftaincy or a leader since a cow is the strongest of the domestic animals.), Cattle also means wealth. In a negative sense, a bull represents worldly government or leadership or a demonic presence or activity (Psa. 22:12 GW, *"Many bulls have surrounded me. Strong bulls from Bashan have encircled me."* This verse was the prophecy of Christ being surrounded by the government of the time when He was on the cross.), a cow also represents a believer it chews its cud (regeneration: a concept of meditation,) and has divided hoofs (sanctification: clean on the outside), see Lev. 11.

Lamb

Christ's sacrifice on the cross or His redemptive work for you, the ultimate Lamb of God (In the midst of the throne in heaven is the Lamb standing, actively working out salvation for us, see Rev. 5:6.). A lamb is a baby sheep, this also means a baby Christian, someone that is still a babe spiritually on the things of the Lord.

Horse

Strength, power, fearlessness, victory (Job 39:19 GW, *"Can you give strength to a horse or dress its neck with a flowing mane?"*). In a negative context the horse means to prepare for battle (Pro. 21:31), putting your trust on vain things (Psa. 33:17), lacking understanding (Psa. 32:9), and one that needs disciplining (Pro. 26:3 KJV, *"A whip for the horse..."*).

Donkey

A servant of the Lord, a journey or assignment that requires no rushing but humility, patience, and consistency. In a negative sense, it means lacking understanding (Psa. 32:9 KJV, *"Be ye not as the horse, or as the mule, which have no understanding..."*), a stubborn person, that which requires control, one who needs to be guided (Pro. 26:3 KJV ...a *bridle for the ass*...).

Snail

Lazy, sluggish, slow progress.

Elephant

Something enormous, heavy, massive, or trouble.

Hippopotamus

Pride, a force of chaos, cosmic evil, without control, unrestrainable.

Jackal

An opportunist, someone who performs menial work.

Rabbit

Someone who flees runs off.

Peacock

Glory, beauty, amazing, extravagant, splendor, colorful.

Dog

If you dream of a dog as belonging to you this dream might be talking about your friend but if you dream of a dog and just don't feel right about it this speaks of a person close to you that is a bad influence. In a positive context, a living dog signifies hope, (Ecc. 9:4 GW, *a living dog is better than a dead lion.*) In a negative context, it signifies hopelessness, (2 Sa. 9:8, *"Mephibosheth bowed down again and answered, "Who am I that you would look at a dead dog like me?"*). Here are other examples of a negative meaning of a dog, uncleanliness (Mat. 7:6 GW, *"Don't give what is holy to dogs"*. In the Jewish concept a dog is unclean both on the inside and the outside, it does not have divided hoofs and cannot chew the cud, see Lev. 11. By this, it means a dog represents someone unclean and an unbeliever.), it also means whoring a dog can mate with its son.

Cat

A female cat that is yours in a dream can mean your girlfriend. On the negative, it means a spiteful or angry woman, jealousy, strife, lust, sexual uncleanliness.

Chicken

A young lady (inexperienced) on the negative it means fear, fright, negligence, carelessness.

Hen

A woman (experienced), (some time ago I was sent a dream from a particular brother, and he dreamt two angry hens and they pecked his face angrily. Interpreted the dream to mean there are two older women fight for his favor (face). The sender of the dream confirmed it as the case.

Cock

That which involves or concerns a male.

Fish

In a positive meaning it signifies a believer, (Luk. 5:10 GW, *"Jesus told Simon, "Don't be afraid. From now on you will catch people instead of fish."*). A lot of fish means a revival or the coming gathering of the Saints in the Lord. Fish without scales means unbeliever(s) (Lev. 11:9 GW, *"Here are the kinds of creatures that live in the water which you may eat-anything in the seas and streams that has fins and scales."*).

Pig

A hypocrite or nominal Christian (it has divided hoofs (a concept of sanctification) but does not chew its cud (a concept of meditation: unrenewed mind), see Lev. 11:7. One who does not value Kingdom principles (Mat. 7:6, *"Don't give what is holy to dogs or throw your pearls to pigs."*), uncleanliness (2 Pet. 2:22 GW, *"A sow that has been washed goes back to roll around in the mud."*).

Stork

Demonic entities, see Zec. 5:6-11.

Zebra

An unstable person (a zebra has yellow and black stripes).

Cheetah

One who habitually sins (a cheetah has spots, biblically spots mean sin). It also means pride.

Giraffe

One lacking courage.

Camel

Represents a minister of God, the preachers of the Word sent to the lost, traveling ministry, itinerant preacher, missionary or evangelist. In the Jewish concept, it is referred to as representing a helper.

Wolf

In a positive meaning, it means rulership, throne generation, kingship posterity, judges of ungodly and oppressive systems (Gen. 49:27, *'Benjamin is a ravenous wolf. In the morning he devours his prey. In the evening he divides the plunder."*). In a negative sense it means the devil as preying on the sheep (believers), a system that steals from people and is greedy, also means false prophets and teachers (Matt. 7:15 KJV, *"Beware of false prophets, which come to you in sheep's clothing, but inwardly they are ravening wolves."*).

Snake

A lie, deception (it is believed by many scholars that a snake was created with outstanding beauty and brilliance, it was shiny, that is why sometimes God can reveal someone who is very intelligent and has a lot of followership in a dream as a snake, this does not many times mean he is evil but that he is used by the devil unaware to deceive many through his/her persuasive oratory abilities, intellectual, brilliance, and charisma, Dr. Mensa Otabil calls such individuals horns which is Hebrew for brilliance and shinning he continues to say, *"A horn blinds people with its brilliance. It appears so superlative, that even the people it subdues think it has a right to subdue them."* These can be political, spiritual people, media influencers, and gurus of some sort. A snake can also mean an evil attack or that which is satanic, see Rev. 12:3-4. When my daughter was 19 months old my wife dreamt three snakes trying to attack her. We vetoed the enemy's plan through prayer. Later my daughter was attacked in 3 areas and all of them, she was not harmed.

Monkey

One that does tricks, swindler, playful,

N.B in ancient times the idols people worshipped were designed to resemble certain animals. The word of God makes it known to us that behind those idols lie demons that people worshipped blindly. To this day when the Lord Opens one to the gift of Discerning of spirits either in a vision or dream (see chapter 6), that individual is more likely to see an animal which animal represents a demon. Let's say you dreamt a frog on top of you. After waking up from such a dream command in this way, *"You _____ (name the spirit, e.g. for a frog it's a spirit of oppression and poverty). I command you to immediately stop with your plots,* *maneuvers, and operations against my life and my families' in Jesus' Name."* Then begin to confess God's promise of that area prone to attack according to the dream. In this case, you'd confess prosperity, wealth, and God's provision for your life. Then only command once and never command again that is what we call resting in God. But you can always confess those promises as much as you want. Below are some of the examples of such spirits.

Leopard

In a positive sense swiftness, agility. In the negative sense of arrogance, pride, or spirit(s) of destruction.

Bear

In a positive sense power and strength (the power and strength of the bear is always paralleled to that of a lion in Scriptures, see 1 Sam. 17:34, Amos 5:19, Hos. 13:8. In a negative sense, it means arrogance, anger, or a spirit of fright.

Frog

It represents demons of oppression, stress, anxiety, depression, financial strain, turmoil, famine, and poverty, and war budget (Rev. 16:13-16).

Scorpion

A lot of scorpions mean a demonic army. A single scorpion means torment (can also be a spirit of torment or death).

Rats

Demonic efforts to steal and corrupt your material gains and wealth.

Insects

Hearing God's voice in Dreams

Flies

Demonic efforts to bring you or the subject of the dream confusion, chaos, and disorder (Mat 12:24 GW, *"When the Pharisees heard this, they said, "This man can force demons out of people only with the help of Beelzebul* (lord of flies), *the ruler of demons."*). Dreaming of dead flies on the oil of a perfume means you are about to be shamed by a little act of foolishness or you are seeing someone that is honored for reputation and wisdom shamed by a little act of foolishness, see Ecc. 10:1.

Bees

In a positive sense, it means the order (from their orderly motion), intuition (based on their systematic instinct), and dedication. In a negative sense it means besieged spiritually (Psa. 118:12 KJV, *"They compassed me about like bees; they are quenched as the fire of thorns: for in the name of the LORD I will destroy them."*), put to fright (Deu. 1:44 KJV, *"...came out against you, and chased you, as bees do..."*).

Ants

In a positive sense, it means hard work, dedication, teamwork, and wisdom (Pro. 6:6 GW, *"Consider the ant, you lazy bum. Watch its ways, and become wise."*). Someone took for granted due to his/her appearance but capable of achieving great things. It also means set out, ready, able to plan and prepare (Pro. 30:25 GW, *"Ants are not a strong species, yet they store their food in summer."*).

Locusts

A nation with no leader (Pro. 30:27 GW, *"Locusts have no king, yet all of them divide into swarms by instinct."*), it also means people who cherish inappropriate conduct and hate deeds of light (locusts sit on fences when it's cold but when the sun comes up they scatter, see Nah. 3:17), demonic spirits that waste harvest, devourers (Amo. 7:2 GW, *"When the locusts had finished eating every plant in*

Hearing God's voice in Dreams

the land, I said, "Almighty LORD, please forgive us! How can the descendants of Jacob survive? There are so few of them."). They also mean worldly armies gathered by the devil (Rev. 9:3 GW, *"Locusts came out of the smoke onto the earth, and they were given power like the power of earthly scorpions."*)

Caterpillar

A demonic force that invades your peace, hope, and rest (Psa. 78:46 KJV, *"He gave also their increase unto the caterpillar,"* they are devourers of the green leaves of the trees, green also means hope or rest).

Cockroach

Sensual people, those led by their senses, fallen people, demonic (cockroaches love darkness but hate light).

Moth

Unclean spirits are demons that influence people with bad character, lasciviousness, and licentiousness (moths eat clothes, clothes in the Scriptural context either mean righteousness, sanctification and holiness or filth, uncleanliness and impurity depending on the context, Job 13:28 GW, *"I am like worn-out wineskins, like moth-eaten clothes."*).

Worm

That which is brought to nothing, emptiness, stripped of everything, useless, hopelessness, a curse or cursed (Job 25:6), death (Job 17:14, Mar. 9:44), devourer, destroyer (Jon. 4:7).

Dung beetle

Dirt, unclean, no sense of direction (dung beetles dig and feed on dung).

Termite(s)

These are the type of insects that consume wood, this means internal sins that cause us to waste from the inside. In such a dream the Lord is revealing any of these internal sins: not walking in love, unbelief, grudges, unforgiveness, jealousy, wrath, anger, hate, envy, etc.

Wasp

A wasp sting, stinging in the New Testament goes alongside the idea of death, see 1 Cor. 15: 55-56). A force of darkness (demon) working to bring about death (sin, sickness, or a disease).

Hearing God's voice in Dreams

Body Parts in Dreams

Head

A leader, a father in a family, preeminence (Christ is the head of the Church Body of Christ, and all we are members of the Body, see Eph. 1:22-23).

Hair

Your cares and concerns, thoughts and meditations for women can also mean your glory (1 Cor. 11:15 GW, *"Doesn't it teach you that it is a woman's pride to wear her hair long? Her hair is given to her in place of a covering."*).

Forehead

From an unused Hebrew root word meaning to be clear, conspicuous, open and prominent, and impudent. Also consider boldness, a stern choice, unwavering, unafraid, mind made up (Eze. 3:9 KJV, *"As an adamant harder than flint have I made thy forehead: fear them not, neither be dismayed at their looks, though they be a rebellious house."*). In a negative sense, it means without courage, unsure, indecisive, confused, and fearful.

Eyes

Window to the soul (Mat. 6:23), spiritual perception, insight, vision, something revealed.

Ears

Spiritual comprehension, obedience to God, understanding of spiritual things (Rev. 2:7 GW, *"Let the person who has ears listen to what the Spirit says to the churches."*). An earring of gold means an obedient person, see Pro. 25:12. Dreaming of a pierced ear means the Lord's bondservant, bound to your master for life (Deu. 15:17 GW, *"Then take an awl and pierce it through his ear lobe into a door, and he will be your slave for life. Do the same to a female slave if she doesn't want to leave."*).

Nose

Temper, anger, wrath (the Hebrew word for the nose is *aph* the same word used for anger and wrath).

Mouth

The mouth is the Hebrew word *peh* which means influence, command, sound, and portion. In a negative sense, it carries the idea of blowing, puffing, to scatter.

Teeth

Side teeth mean your ability to meditate. Teeth also mean to teach diligently or to teach by repeated instruction (from the Hebrew root *Shanan*), front teeth mean sharp or to point. In a negative sense they mean to prick, to pierce, or a cliff as in the idea of a steep or hardness.

Tongue

That which concerns speech, words, and confession, blessing, cursing. It also means spiritual discernment or perception (you taste with your tongue).

Chin/beard

It implies age or growth. Beard also signifies church elders or leadership (Psa. 133:1-3).

Neck

Binding, connector, mediator, or meeting point (it connects the head and the body). In a negative sense it means where the burdens are placed, burdens, loads, unrest, troubled, perplexed.

Shoulder(s)

To be responsible to carry out something, accountable and answer to someone or for something, carry, to share a burden, take something upon yourself, your portion, share of something (Isa. 9:6 GW, *"A child will be born for us. A son will be given to us. The government will rest on his shoulders."*). In a negative context, it means an overload, slavery, overworked, overused.

Hand

Power, the handle of something, this also applies to the palm of a hand/open hand.

Closed hand

Disconnected, inaccessible, unreceptive.

Right hand

Your exercise or position of authority (Act 2:34 GW, *"David didn't go up to heaven, but he said, 'The Lord said to my Lord, "Take my highest position of power."*"), long life (Pro. 3:16), a place of blessing, inheritance, and honor (Mat. 25:33-34 GW, *"He will put the sheep on his right but the goats on his left." Then the king will say to those on his right, 'Come, my Father has blessed you! Inherit the kingdom prepared for you from the creation of the world."*).

Left hand

That which is in your power to do, riches and honor (Pro. 3:16 GW, *"In wisdom's left hand are riches and honor."*), disallowed and dishonor (Mat. 25:41 GW, *"Then the king will say to those on his left, 'Get away from me! God has cursed you! Go into everlasting fire that was prepared for the devil and his angels!"*).

Arm

Your position, place of influence, God-given office (1 Sa. 2:31 GW, *"Behold, the days come, that I will cut off thine arm, and *the arm of thy father's house, that there shall not be an old man in thine house."*).

Hand

Power, might, to accept, your work (ability). Open hand means your capacity to receive or that you are open to receive from God. Closed hand means your being unreceptive, unopen, or unaccepting.

Chest

Personal inner thoughts, one's secret feelings, desires. It also means bosom, warmth, to lean on (trust), a place of comfort, and consolation.

Stomach

The spirit man inside the body (Pro. 20:27, Joh. 4:14 & 7:37-38), the capacity to keep secrets, courage (having guts), satisfaction, appetite, womb (Jer. 1:5), pleasure. In a negative sense, it means gluttony, unsatisfactory, unable to keep secrets, cowardice.

Back

It has to do with the past things of your life that which is behind, giving a blind eye to something, choosing to avoid.

Fingers: (See, Ephesians 4:11)

1. **Thumb:** the toughest and the strongest finger, the office of an Apostle.
2. **Forefinger:** the pointing finger, the office of a Prophet.
3. **Middle finger:** the longest of all the fingers, the office of an Evangelist.
4. **Second finger:** it balances the fingers of the hand, the office of a Pastor.

5. **Pinky/smallest finger:** it reaches places that other fingers can't, like cleaning an ear, the office of a Teacher.

Loins

Preparedness, readiness, about to hasten, many times in the Bible the word refers to the organ of generations (descendants, posterity, generational blessing, and inheritance, Heb. 7:9-10 KJV, *"And as I may so say, Levi also, who receiveth tithes, paid tithes in Abraham. For he was yet in the loins of his father, when Melchisedec met him."*).

Thigh

Truth, honesty, oath, a vow (in Bible times people would seal a promise among each other by having the other place his hand under the other's thigh, Gen. 24:2 KJV, *"And Abraham said unto his eldest servant of his house, that ruled over all that he had, Put, I pray thee, thy hand under my thigh."*, see also Gen. 47:29.

Buttocks

Shame, stripped, undignified, dishonor, disrespect (Isa. 20:4 KJV, *"So shall the king of Assyria lead away from the Egyptians prisoners, and the Ethiopians captives, young and old, naked and barefoot, even with their buttocks uncovered, to the shame of Egypt."*), see also, 1 Ch. 19:4.

Private parts

Personal secrets, hidden things.

Knees

Your prayer life, humility, and humbleness. In the negative, it means to tremble or weaken.

Legs

Hearing God's voice in Dreams

Bravery (Psa. 147:10 KJV, *"He delighteth not in the strength of the horse: he taketh not pleasure in the legs of a man."* God's Word translation puts it, *"...nor is he pleased by brave soldiers."*), strength (legs are the strongest members of the body, they carry the entire weight of the upper body), your integrity to fulfill your promises.

Feet

Your walk in the Lord, your standing, your position, it also implies your coming in and going out (This is what John has to say about Jesus Christ's feet, *"His feet were glowing like bronze being heated in a furnace,"* vs.15 CEV. Bronze is like gold in appearance except that it is shinier than gold and at the same time, heavier than gold, bronze in one's feet would cause one to walk slowly since it's heavy. The Lord Jesus' message here is that He is coming again but slowly and patiently that people may still have time to repent and turn to Him).

Toes

Your walk of obligation (ten toes).

Blood

That which concerns life and soul. Dreaming of blood may also be a prediction of death.

Skeleton

Hopelessness, despair, defeat, failure, scattered (see Ezekiel 37).

Places/Buildings in Dreams

Home

What is currently happening in your life, issues concerning your security, comfort, and an **old home** represents your past life, memory, or unresolved issues.

Field

Evangelistic work, outreach ministry.

Farm

A place where you are required to take initiative to bring out results, fruits or produce. It also means a ministry outside of the church, it can be evangelism. A place of provision.

Valley

A place of death, suffering, or a place of decision.

Island

A secluded individual, a solitary one. It also means desire or longing.

Stadium

Massive impact, great influence, mass evangelism.

Desert

A dry place, drought, a time of testing.

Elevator

God taking you to the next level of your life can be spiritually, emotionally, financially, etc. without your effort. If it is going down it means you are regressing from the things of faith.

Staircase

God taking you to the next level of your life one step at a time, it can be spiritually, financially, or emotionally, etc. but for Him to do this, it will require your effort. If you are going down it means you are regressing from the elements of faith one step at a time.

Cafeteria

Being positioned to petition or request according to your needs demand (in a cafeteria customers order and select their food at a counter).

Restaurant

To be or about to be served, ministered to (in a restaurant you are served on your table), this emphatically means being positioned to receive answers to your prayers.

Office

The sphere or nature of your calling, your God-given ministry in the fivefold (Apostle, Prophet, Evangelist, Pastor, Teacher, see Eph. 4:11).

Building

This means a place God has put you or taking you to, a situation. A building is different from a house see the meaning of a house below. A high building means a higher spiritual calling.

Double story house

Double anointing, double responsibility, double impact, more accountability.

Hospital

Healing ministry, divine healing, the ministry of laying hands on the sick and they recover. In a negative sense, it points to a place of the broken (emotionally, financially, or spiritually).

Gymnasium

A place of growth spiritually and mentally.

Park

A place of temporary rest, to take a break from your daily labor, to relax for a while to resume back to your responsibilities, family enjoyment time.

Construction site

Somewhere in God's plan and purpose you should be but the Lord is still preparing, God, working not yet finished about something along with your destiny, the need for you to trust Him and be patient with Him.

Scrapyard

A ministry raised for broken and hurting believers.

Tent

Temporary situation or rest.

Temple

That which concerns your physical body or work of service in your local church.

Mall

In the mall, it's where you have enough options of what to buy meaning the salvation package (the Greek word for salvation in the New Testament is *Sozo* which means salvation, deliverance, health, wholeness, prosperity, and abundance). It also means the

Kingdom a place of unlimited resources and supply. It also means the marketplace. On the negative it means materialism.

Casino

Entertainment, fleshly pleasure, amusement. It also means risking in hope of a potential gain.

Filling Station/gas station

This is where cars go for gas refilling therefore this means your place of fellowship (church) where all ministries (lives) are empowered and equipped.

Warehouse

It means a place of storage and provision. It can also mean deep things of the heart, thoughts of the soul (emotions).

Poultry

Young women's ministry, a place of delivering the fruits of the womb (gifts) and where they also need to be incubated.

Prison

It means addiction or spiritual oppression.

Zoo

A wilderness experience, a trial experience, strange.

Circus

A place of fleshly entertainment, of the lust of the eye, enticement, soulish cravings, showmanship, or chaos.

Theatre

God has made you an exhibition, someone or some people is watching your life (1 Cor. 4:9 GW, "*As I see it, God has placed us apostles last in line, like people condemned to die. We have become a spectacle for people and angels to look at."*). It can also mean a display.

Repair shop

God is either bringing you to a place of restoration, refreshing, or of renewal or God wants you to restore someone or certain people or something.

Shack

A temporary situation or poverty, destitution, lack of resources.

Bridge

Transition (in a process or about to be moved by God from one place in your life to another), change, transformation.

Tunnel

Breakthrough, acceleration, or quick transition.

Hallway

God moving you through a direct process from one place to another within a short time.

Garden

God's presence (God planted a garden in Eden, the word Eden means God's Presence, Isaiah 61:11b GW, *"and like a garden that makes the seed in it grow, so the Almighty LORD will make righteousness and praise spring up in front of all nations."*). It can also mean your love life, your partner, especially your marital sex life (Son. 6:2 GW, [Bride] *"My beloved went to his garden, to the beds of spices, to graze his flock in the gardens and gather lilies."*).

Graveyard

A place of buried potentials, dead gifts, despair, lack of hope.

Classroom

A teaching ministry. It can also mean a particular lesson God wants to teach you, something God wants you to learn.

N.B There are three levels of growth in the Christian life. In dreams, they can be expressed as the primary/elementary school, secondary/high school, and the tertiary level. See below:

Primary School

God wanting or willing to establish you in elementary teachings of the Kingdom (such teachings as walking in love, faith, the gifts of the Spirit, baptisms, laying on of hands, the resurrection from the dead and touching eternal judgment, see Heb. 6:1-2). Dreaming yourself going back to elementary school may mean you are repeating the same mistake in your life and there is a lesson you need to learn out of it. It also means regressing to issues of the flesh, being led by the senses, or back to basics.

Secondary School

The second level of spiritual growth (Rom. 8:20-21 GW, *"Creation was subjected to frustration but not by its own choice. The one who subjected it to frustration did so in the hope that it would also be set free from slavery to decay to share the glorious freedom that the children of God will have."*). The child level Greek *teknon* meaning a child or children. This is the level of introduction to teachings of justification by faith, righteousness, understanding the glorious liberty of the children of God, discernment, and exercising of spiritual senses. Going back to secondary school means making the same mistakes again concerning faith and righteousness foundations.

University/College

God willing and wanting you established in the level of Sonship (Joh. 1:12 KJV, *"But as many as received him, to them gave He power to become the sons of God, even to them that believe on his name."* Emphasis added.). This is the level of maturity in teachings of righteousness, justification by faith, salvation, redemption, and Christ's finished work, Heb. 5:13 KJV, *"For every one that useth milk is unskilful in the word of righteousness: for he is a babe."*).

House

A **house** means you personally, your life, (2 Ki. 20:1 KJV, *"In those days was Hezekiah sick unto death. And the prophet Isaiah the son of Amoz came to him, and said unto him, Thus saith the LORD, Set thine house in order; for thou shalt die, and not live."*). It can also be about your family (Gen. 31:30 KJV, *"And now, though thou wouldest needs be gone, because thou sore longest after thy father's house, yet wherefore hast thou stolen my gods?"*).

Bedroom

Intimate thoughts, heart's desires, prayer life, your place of rest.

Bathroom

Sanctification, a place of cleansing.

Kitchen

Your call or that which concerns your serving, servanthood, preparing.

Dining room

A place of communion, interacting, gathering, fellowship, welcoming, a place of receiving. In the negative, it means a place of commotion, noise, or sound.

Front porch

The future, seeing ahead.

Balcony

A bigger vision or the need to stretch forth, going big.

Garage

Where a car (gift, calling) is on hold, suspended, parked, where a ministry is paused.

Backyard

Your life or family's history or past. It can also mean what you disregard or devalue, what you take for granted.

Front yard

Your life or family's future. It can also mean what you prioritize, what you value and esteem highly, and also means prominence.

Playground

Playfulness, unserious. It can sometimes mean that what you take for fun God will use it to bring about something good out of you, to train you.

Lawn

That which you hold dear to your life, what is precious to your life.

Outside the house

This means the world, outside the Kingdom of God.

Window

A revelation, insight, vision, or spiritual enlightenment. An open window means God opening you to receive a revelation or spiritual insight. Looking out the window means God revealing something to you.

Door

An opportunity. A closed door is a closed opportunity and an open door is an open opportunity. It also means the human spirit, heart (Rev. 3:20 GW, *"Look, I'm standing at the door and knocking. If anyone listens to my voice and opens the door, I'll come in and we'll eat together."*). A spiritual opening, portal, see Rev. 4:1.

Roof

Spiritual covering.

Floor/Foundation

Beliefs, convictions, values, foundational doctrines, church leadership, or government.

Pillars

Wisdom (Prov. 9:1 GW, *"Wisdom has built her house. She has carved out her seven pillars."*). An essential part of your life or what gives you support.

Walls

Protection, that which concerns your in-laws or family. It also means a mental fortitude.

Fireplace

Your prayer closet, prayer life.

Keys

Principles, authority (Mat. 16:19 GW, *"I will give you the keys of the kingdom of heaven. Whatever you imprison, God will imprison. And whatever you set free, God will set free."*).

Gate

Leadership, counsel, advisory position, prestige, influential position in a community, dominion (Gen. 22:17 KJV, *"That in blessing I will bless thee, and in multiplying I will multiply thy seed as the stars of the heaven, and as the sand which is upon the seashore; and thy seed shall possess the gate of his enemies."*). Something you have allowed and have the power to reject, the ability to loose Kingdom conditions and blessings.

Restroom

A place of ridding off unwanted things in your life and toxic things.

Basement

Hidden things and your secrecies.

Storeroom

A place of provision. It can also mean a place of storage or your mind or heart.

Shade

A shade or a shadow means defense.

Household Essentials

Electricity

The miracle-working power, supernatural power, anointing, Holy Spirit's power, *"Electricity is God's power in the natural realm, but the Holy Ghost power is God's power in the spirit realm."* – John G. Lake.

Light (bulb)

Light of the Word of God, knowledge of the Word about a particular situation, what you have an ability to dispel through the Word. It can also mean something exposed.

Cooking stove

A process of preparation that requires one to undergo intense pressure. It also means your prayer life in the line of prayers of surrendering or it can mean God expects you to do something that will create a lot of heat around it (to be bad mouthed, persecuted, or tried).

Pot

A situation. A boiling pot means trouble (Jer. 1:13-14 GW, *"Again the LORD spoke his word to me and asked, "What do you see?" I answered, "I see a boiling pot, and its top is tilted away from the north." Then the LORD said to me, "Disaster will be poured out from the north on all those who live in the land."*).

Vessels

God's called-out ones, God's servants in ministry (2 Ti. 2:20 ASV, *"Now in a great house there are not only vessels of gold and silver, but also of wood and earth; and some unto honor, and some unto dishonor."* See also, Rom. 9:23.).

Cup

Blessing(s), curse(s), partaking, oneness (1 Cor. 10:21), the wrath of God (Rev. 16:19).

Spoon

Stirring something, awaken and excite. In the negative, it means to disturb provoke, incite, and rouse.

Tray

To serve especially, something prepared for especially, a special treat.

Table

Being served, being taken care of, favor or favored, goodwill, supplied for, provision.

Chair

Resuming a position, settle, calm, or being established.

Sofa

Comfort, cushioned, contentment, ease, relief.

Curtain

A veil, something hidden, uncovered, unveiled.

Mirror

The Word of God (Jas. 1:23-24 GW, *"If someone listens to God's word but doesn't do what it says, he is like a person who looks at his face in a mirror, studies his features, goes away, and immediately forgets what he looks like."*).

Toaster

Putting under intense pressure (see a cooking stove).

Blanket

Warmth, covered, enclosed.

Iron

That which straightens things out, rearranging matters of your life.

Washing machine

Where you do away with dirt (removing character stains, flaws, and inconsistencies). It is also our reviewing of our walk of faith or of the things we have been doing especially the ones inconsistent with the Word of God.

Microwave

To refresh a course, situation, or service. To revive, revitalize your passion, dedication, and devotion to the Lord.

Television

Being shown a vision in a dream, something revealed to you.

Sound System

An orderly arrangement of things, order, the absence of chaos.

Personal Devices/Items

Mobile phone

Dreaming of a call or S.M.S means a message or calling that is personally directed to you. A matter that will require obedience.

Radio

A message that is mass directed, can involve a nation, community, church, or people. It is therefore meant to be shared and will require obedience from the intended people.

Personal Computer

A P.C was originally invented for businesses and then it evolved to be a household device. It is used for storing data, programming, processing, performing mathematical calculations, etc. This, therefore, is a revelation of the mind pattern prevailing in your family governing your approach to business, workplace, and principles of productivity, their perceptions, imaginations, and ideas.

Laptop

A laptop is more like a digitized notebook, it is a computer that is flexible to carry it anywhere. It means a revelation of your mind or someone else's concerning their thought processes, decisions, logic, ideas, perceptions, and imaginations.

Wallet/Purse

Your capacity to receive or your ability to carry what you have been blessed with.

Picture

It means idolizing something, illusion, it can also mean imagination. Looking at yourself in a picture reveals a need to change how you see yourself, the perception you have of yourself.

Bag pack

Luggage, responsibility, load, or burden.

Handbag

Glory or favor can also reveal your level of expectation or receiving capacity.

Makeup

How you present yourself to people, how you appropriate your God-given favor, concealment, or pretense. Makeup was also used in the Bible as early as four thousand years before Christ came to earth. In Job's restoration God gave him three daughters who were the most beautiful in the whole land, the youngest was called Keren-happuch, which means a cosmetic jar also known as a box of eye paint, more precisely a container for black powder used like modern mascara, Job 42:14.

Perfume

Reputation, a good name or honor, influence, excellence, beauty. Job's second daughter's name was called Keziah meaning a precious perfume, Job 42:14 & Ps. 45:9.

Necklace

Charm, to impress, ravish, to capture a heart (Son. 9:4 GW, *"My bride, my sister, you have charmed me. You have charmed me with a single glance from your eyes, with a single strand of your necklace."*), it also reveals one's level of discipline and foundational teachings (values), example a gold necklace reveals good discipline and teachings (Pro. 1:9 GW, *"because discipline and teachings are a graceful garland on your head and a golden chain around your neck."*).

Wristwatch

Your commitment to God's timing.

Diary

Details concerning your past experiences, that which concerns your past life experiences.

Pen

Words of the mouth, confession (Psa. 45:1 GW, *"My heart is overflowing with good news. I will direct my song to the king. My tongue is a pen for a skillful writer."*).

Ring

Love life, Marriage commitment, your covenant in Christ.

Umbrella

Covering, ministry.

Roads in Dreams

Highway

A path of life (Prov. 16:17), a revelation of the Divine glory of God upon your life to all the world. A highway through river and desert means a miraculous passage or a restoration from lost resources and confinement (Isa. 11:16). A highway also means a high-speed road which means your need to pace up concerning what you are called for, a public ministry, a very busy calling.

Upper/high road

A ministry that will be well known, exaltation.

City roads

Driving on city roads has to do with the scope of your calling and destiny in view of the political, social, and technical development of your nation.

Local roads

Your calling and destiny in view of the area revealed the context of the dream is important to find a substantiated meaning.

One lane

A journey of ease will not have objects to slow you down.

Two lanes

A journey of occasional resistance that will sometimes require you to overtake to progress at a consistent and intended acceleration.

Crossroads

At a decision point or offered an opportunity to change direction. It can also mean being confused about the next step to take in your life.

Gravel road

A journey that is testing and will emotionally feel hard to understand and make sense of.

Dead-end

Coming to the end of something, can be an end of service to a certain ministry or business or an end of a particular journey in your life, see the *Preface* to refer to my dead-end dream.

Stop sign

A need to stop and assess before joining a certain course or taking a particular direction in your life.

Traffic lights

Greenlight: it is safe to continue in your journey or it may mean the decision you are about to take is the right decision.

Yellow light: you may proceed with caution in your journey.

Red light: you should stop from proceeding in your journey or God may be denying you of a certain course or decision it also signals a warning.

Straight road

You are in harmony or union with God in your journey, a journey that is right, pleasant, or prosperous, it also means equity, fairness, and justice.

Crooked road

A dishonest, corrupt, illegal journey or experience, a rough journey.

Upslope

A spiritual uplifting that will be emotionally exhausting and challenging.

Downslope

A spiritual downcast.

U-turn

God bringing you to a point in your ministry or calling where you are required to turn in the opposite of that direction or the opposite of your ministry. To turn back.

Sharp right curve

An intense and uncomfortable change in your life and calling in areas pertaining to your spiritual authority, position in Christ, blessings, and inheritance.

Sharp left curve

An intense and uncomfortable change in your life and calling in areas about your power (what you are able to do), material gains, and honor.

Smooth right curve

An easy and comfortable change in your life and calling in areas pertaining to your spiritual authority, position in Christ, blessings, and inheritance.

Smooth left curve

An easy and comfortable change in your life and calling in areas about your power (what you are able to do), material gains, and honor.

Off-ramp

The need to discontinue in your journey and take the shortest way possible, the need to change the course of your ministry or destiny.

Nature in Dreams

Sun

The ultimate light of our galaxy. It means Christ as the ultimate Light and glory of all mankind.

Moon

The lesser light. The moon receives its light from the light of the sun, it, therefore, reflects the sun's light. This refers to the Body of Christ, the Church. As believers, we exhibit Christ's life and glory.

Stars

Glory, God's saints (Dan. 12:3), angels (Job 38:7, Rev. 12:4).

Cloud

The saints who have gone before us (Heb. 12:1 Darby, *"Let *us* also, therefore, having so great a cloud of witnesses surrounding us, laying aside every weight, and sin which so easily entangles us, run with endurance the race that lies before us."* This verse comes directly after the hall of faith, the 19 great names of the Old Testament saints mentioned in Hebrews 11). A cloud is also one of the attributes of the presence of the Holy Spirit's leadership, see Exo. 13:21).

Lightning

God's glory (Dan. 10:6), what God will perform speedily, supernatural acceleration (Eze. 1:14), the Second coming of Christ (Matt. 24:27). It also means judgment or scattering (Zec. 9:14, Isa. 144:6).

Rainbow

Everlasting promise, covenant, oath (Gen. 9:13 GW, *"I will put my rainbow in the clouds to be a sign of my promise to the earth."*).

Thunder

Judgment (Exo. 9:23 GW, *"When Moses lifted his staff toward the sky, the LORD sent thunder and hail, and lightning struck the earth. So the LORD made it hail on Egypt."*).

Fire

The Holy Spirit's power (Lk. 3:16), God's judgment (Ps. 78:21), trials (Ps. 66:12). Sparks of fire mean trouble (Job 5:7).

Mountain

Kingdom, a place of exaltation (Dan. 2:44-45), problems, distraction, limitation, or obstacle (Mar. 11:23).

Grass

Sustenance and provision for the sheep and herds (believers), see Psa. 23:2. Material things, works of man, that which fades away, what does not last (Psa. 37:2).

Hyssop

Means faith, it's a small plant growing out of walls a picture of little faith capable of impossibilities (Exo. 12:22), it also means the precious peace of the recreated spirit (Ps. 51:7).

Flower

Blooming, flourishing, goodliness. On the negative, it means the glory of man (1 Pet. 1:24) or that which withers away.

Reed

Carried away by every kind of doctrine, lacking Christian character, unstable, easily shaken, deceived, flattered (Eph. 4:14).

Valley

A place of testing, a place of striving, hardship, and temptation (Gen. 14:8), or it can mean a place of decision (Joe 3:14).

Forest

Alone, deserted, desolate, abandoned a place of trials, wilderness. Trees in the forest also mean a lot of people, unbelievers. It also means the world (Jos. 17:15 & 18).

Cave

A hiding place, refugee, Christ.

Rain

Heavenly provision, God's goodness, a blessing, God's supply.

Drought

A dry season, famine, insufficiency, in need, lack.

Fog

What quickly disappears (Hos. 6:4), boasting, a false gift (Pro. 25:14 GW, *"Like a dense fog or a dust storm, so is a person who brags about a gift that he does not give."*).

Mist

Human life span (Jas. 4:14), nature of false teaching, and false teachers (2 Pet. 2:17). It also means what quickly disappears (Isa. 44:22 GW, *"I made your rebellious acts disappear like a thick cloud and your sins like the morning mist. Come back to me, because I have reclaimed you."*).

Frost

The Hebrew word for frost comes from the root word *kaphar* which means to expiate, atone (the Old Testament concept for sins covered by animal blood), forgive, merciful, appease, and put off, reconciliation, pardon, cancel. In the negative it means destruction (Psa. 78:47), it also means what quickly disappears.

Dew

Increase, multiplication, fertility, favor, the blessing, God's goodness (Gen. 27:28 GW, *"May God give you dew from the sky, fertile fields on the earth, and plenty of fresh grain and new wine."* Psa. 133:3 GW, *"It is like dew on Mount Hermon, dew which comes down on Zion's mountains. That is where the LORD promised the blessing of eternal life."*).

Snow

Redemption, sanctification (cleansing), purification, see Isa. 1:18. The Word of God that produces results (Isa. 55:11 GW, *"My word, which comes from my mouth, is like the rain and snow. It will not come back to me without results. It will accomplish whatever I want and achieve whatever I send it to do."*).

Storm

God's anger (Job 36:33, GW *"...The storm announces his angry wrath."*). A commotion brought by the enemy.

Wind

One of the characteristics of the Holy Spirit. Unfavorable conditions (Ecc. 11:4). It also means vanity, emptiness, and vexation of spirit (Ecc. 6:9b GW, *"...Even this is pointless. It's like trying to catch the wind."*).

Hail

Destruction and judgment (Exo. 9:22 GW, *"Then the LORD said to Moses, "Lift your hand toward the sky, and hail will fall on people, animals, and every plant in the fields of Egypt."*).

Flood

Defense and fortitude of the Holy Spirit, Isa. 59:19 KJV, *"So shall they fear the name of the LORD from the west, and his glory from the rising of the sun. When the enemy shall come in like a flood, the Spirit of the LORD shall lift a standard against him."* The Hebrew language has no commas but uses emphasis, on the above verse the comma should be after 'in', *when the enemy shall come in, like the flood the Spirit of the Lord shall lift a standard against him*. The flood should be associated with the Spirit of God not with the enemy. This intimates that the standard is raised by the Lord. Flood also means satanic invasion and swift destruction, see Jer. 46:8.

Earthquake

Terrifying, the shaking of kingdoms or systems (Mat. 27:54 GW, *"An army officer and those watching Jesus with him saw the earthquake and the other things happening. They were terrified and said, "Certainly, this was the Son of God!"*).

Light

God's Word, works of righteousness (Psa. 119:105 GW, *"Your word is a lamp for my feet and a light for my path."*).

Darkness

Mysteries of God (Psa. 18:11 GW, *"He made the darkness his hiding place."*). Works of darkness, devilish activity (Lk. 22:53 GW, *"I was with you in the temple courtyard every day and you didn't try to arrest me. But this is your time when darkness rules."*).

Land

Earth, common, field, world, earthy.

Ground

Heart(s) or the believer's life, see Mar. 4:14-20.

Sand

People, earthly glory, fame, seeking people's approval, fleshly motives (Mat. 7:26-27 GW, *"Everyone who hears what I say but doesn't obey it will be like a foolish person who built a house on sand. Rain poured, and floods came. Winds blew and struck that house. It collapsed, and the result was a total disaster."*).

Clay

Nothingness, abase, unworthiness, the nature of the human fall, weak, fragile. On the positive side, it means God molding you in line with His purpose and will (Isa. 64:8 GW, *"But now, LORD, you are our Father. We are the clay, and you are our potter. We are the work of your hands."*).

Seed

The Word of God (prophetic or the written Word) requires action from your part to initiate its process since a seed requires you to plant it before it can grow.

Tree

Your life's work, empire, work, job, marketplace influence, or ministerial (Psa. 1:1a & 3 GW, *"Blessed is the person who does not follow the advice of wicked people, ...He is like a tree planted beside streams- a tree that produces fruit in season and whose leaves do not wither. He succeeds in everything he does."* See also Jer. 17:7-8. It also means family, see Job 18:16 in this case branches speak of children.

Myrrh

Speaks of death, it exudes its fragrance by crushing. Trials by the result of the cross that is able to bring out glory in us.

Cinnamon

Comes from the Hebrew *Kinna* meaning "jealousy" and *min* meaning "the appearance of", "the appearance of jealousy." It mainly means Christ's divine jealousy over us.

Sweet calamus

It's a reed or cane, in Hebrew it means "stand upright." This signifies our position of righteousness in Christ.

Cassice

Means "stoop or bow down," speaks of worship. King of Tyre trafficked in Cassice (Eze. 27:19 & 28:18, Satan is the king of Tyre referred to).

Apple Tree

Pleasant, dear, loved person (Son. 2:3 GW, *"[Bride] Like an apple tree among the trees in the forest, so is my beloved among the young men. I want to sit in his shadow. His fruit tastes sweet to me."*).

Wood

That which is human, man's corruptible nature, Adam's nature (wood decays, God in instructing Moses He told him to use the acacia wood in the Tabernacle and the Ark of the Covenant, the acacia wood could not be eaten by termites and does not corrupt, a picture of Christ in an incorruptible nature). See 1 Cor. 3:12.

Hay

The works or products of man's fallen nature that which comes from man and cannot please God, his (man's) cursed nature. See 1 Cor. 3:12.

Stubble

The weaknesses of man, the deadness, uselessness of the natural life, see 1 Cor. 3:12.

Hearing God's voice in Dreams

Bitter herbs

Being given bitter herbs or eating them means about to experience suffering, if having a physical ailment and dream eating bitter herbs or being given bitter herbs it means supernatural healing (on the Passover feast the Israelites ate their meal with bitter herbs a picture of Christ's suffering on the cross, His emotional and physical sufferings that we may also be healed physically).

Fruits

Fruits of the human spirit in a believer's life, see Gal. 5:22-23. The works of righteousness, fruitfulness. Fruits have seeds in them this means a harvest whose longevity is determined by you. When you eat a fruit you are required to set aside the seed, this means God is showing you in your season of plenty you need not to forget to sow, eat and sow, don't also devour the seed.

All the sweet fruits represent a pleasant experience like **peach**, **apricot**, **strawberry**, **fig**, etc. When they are unripe they become sour representing an unfavorable experience. **Watermelon** is bigger than normal fruits meaning an abundance of favor and pleasantness. **Pomegranate** means to rise, to be exalted, glorified, **olive** means brightness, to be prominent after crushing (pain), **grapes,** mean restoration, reinstating, compensation, redemptive work. **Cucumber** as one of the fruits means work of your labors, a cucumber garden means in the presence of or among people, see Isa.1:8 and Jer. 10:5.

More than two different fruit trees may mean being offered a choice.

Vegetables

Labor or service of man (Psa. 104:14 KJV, *"He causeth the grass to grow for the cattle, and herb* (*eseb* the Hebrew word for vegetables) *for the service of man: that he may bring forth food out of the earth."*). They also mean to glisten, excel, radiate or outshine.

N.B Vegetables are edible plants, there are three types of them:
1. The ones that are leaves (such as spinach, cabbage, lettuce, etc.).
2. The ones that are roots (carrot, onion, potato, etc.).
3. The ones that are seed themselves (tomato, etc.).

Edible leaves vegetables: in the edible leaves vegetables we have two types, the ones that can be eaten raw and the ones that need to be cooked. The ones that can be eaten raw such as **lettuce** represent God's promise(s) to you, leaves are the first sign of harvest, dreaming eating lettuce might mean it is your time to be satisfied with God's promise(s). You don't have to do anything to enjoy God's promise(s) but only believing no effort is needed. Edible leaves vegetables that require to be cooked before eating represent God's conditional prophecy over your life such as **cabbage, spinach**, etc., you cannot eat these without cooking them they, therefore, require some effort on your part before enjoying them. This means your season of harvesting the prophecies released upon your life by God through the Holy Spirit (dreams, visions, or inspiration) or God's servants, the prophets have come but you won't be able to enjoy the season provided you obey what you were told to do to see those prophecies come to pass. In the case of Elijah, he was promised to enjoy God's provision in the face of the national drought provided he went to the brook of Cherith, see 1 Ki. 17:3-4, and later go to Zarephath, see 1 Ki. 17:8-9. If Elijah had decided to not go to any of those places he could have starved to death.

Edible roots vegetables: most of the edible roots vegetables require cooking such as **carrot, onion, potato, sweet potato, beetroot**, etc. Carrot can also be eaten raw, dreaming eating it raw represents a generational blessing meaning a generational blessing that requires no effort on your part to be released on your family or generation but only requires faith. These types of vegetables represent God's generational blessing, your family blessings, and posterity blessings. In the Bible roots represent generations or a family course, Isa 11:1 GW, *"Then a shoot will come out from the* *stump of Jesse, and a branch from its roots will bear fruit."* See also Daniel 11:7.

Edible seeds vegetables: they mostly require cooking also such as a **tomato**. It can also be eaten raw. Eating it raw in a dream means a soon to manifest once offseason of harvest over your life that requires only faith on your part but no effort. Eating it cooked means your need to put some effort to see the once offseason of harvest on your life fulfilled. Edible seeds vegetables are seeds on their own without carrying a seed inside when you eat them you have also eaten a seed, this means a non to recur season of harvest in your life. This helps to guide you in wisdom, example: Let's assume you have a part-time business and have a day job and it happens you have a dream of eating a rich tomato and it so happens your business hits an overnight success and you are tempted to quit your day job to focus on your business. This might mean God was warning you not to quit your day job yet because your experienced business success was a once-off seasonal harvest. You always have to rely on the context of the dream, if you dream of selling tomatoes or any of the edible seeds vegetables it means something different from the above definition, it can mean any of the following, to sow and scatter principles (a teaching ministry), ideas and opinions (the spirit of counsel) for growth or propagation (winning new converts) or to help others conceive (people realize their gifts). Tomato can also mean a fruit of the womb.

Melon, onion, leek, and **garlic** were diets of the lower classes according to the Bible, see Num. 11:5. Onion in the Bible comes from the root word peel which represents success requiring effort to enjoy and garlic comes from the root word exhale due to its rank odor this means an offensive or intense experience.

Let's recap, edible leaf vegetables represent God's promises, edible roots vegetables represent generational blessings and edible seeds vegetables represent a once offseason of harvest.

Vine

The life of Christ is expressed in the Church. The vine represents the life of Christ and the branches represent the believers engrafted into Christ's life. See Joh. 15.

Mustard seed

The mustard seed is the smallest seed about the size of a seed of rice which when it grows becomes the biggest tree in the field. It represents the measure of faith that God has given all believers (Rom. 12:3) which can grow to unprecedented heights.

Corn

Food provision, the season of harvest. The cornfield means the Kingdom of God (Matt. 13:24).

Olive tree

A symbol of reconciliation and peace. It also means to be prominent.

Palm tree

Upright (righteousness), reaching broadly upwards, standing out.

Fig tree

A sign that summer, a jubilant, rejoicing and celebration season or harvest is near (as soon as its branches are tender it marks that summer is around the corner), it also marks the sign of the end times, Israel and that the end of all things is near, see Mat. 24:32-35. On the negative side it means hypocrisy, it is the only tree that can put forth fruit before leaves or sometimes may produce fruits and leaves at the same time (Mar. 11:13 KJV, *"And seeing a fig tree afar off having leaves, he came, if haply he might find anything thereon: and when he came to it, he found nothing but leaves; for the time of figs was not yet."*).

Thornbush (bramble)

Sin, the fall, or the curse as a result of the fall (in the Bible we find the thorn bush when Moses sees it burning, a picture of God judging sin). The Hebrew word for thorn bush means to prick, meaning to persecute, offend or incite.

Thorn

A curse, hindrance, offense. Because of Adam's fall, cursed was the ground his body was formed from, it produced thistles and thorns for him (Gen. 3:18-19). When the man would try to plant seeds in the field thorns would prick him this meant that the unseen forces acted against him rather than for him. On the cross, Christ was crowned with thorns.

Stone

The chief cornerstone being Christ (1 Pet. 2:6), the lively or precious stones being believers (1 Pet. 2:5). On the negative side, it means the hardness of the heart or the heart of the unbelieving.

Rock

Christ the protector (Gen. 49:24 GW, "...*because of the name of the Shepherd, the Rock of Israel.*" And 1 Cor. 10:4 KJV, "...*for they drank of that spiritual Rock that followed them: and that Rock was Christ.*").

Shapes

Triangle

The God shape representing trinity, agreement, unity on the negative side it represents controversy, against, imbalance, inability, and what is limited.

Rectangle

That which represents the whole wide world, the world (Rev. 7:1 GW, *"After this, I saw four angels standing at the four corners of the earth. They were holding back the four winds of the earth to keep them from blowing on the land, the sea, or any tree."* According to this verse, John perceived the earth as standing upon the four corners, a rectangle shape the Hebrew concept of North, East, South, and West. We have to keep in mind that John is looking down upon the earth from heaven, seeing it as a plane). The world has four elements earth, fire, water, and air, four cardinal points N.E.S.W and four seasons.

Square

The level of attainment, God's standard and measure of righteousness (Eze. 43:16 GW, *"It was square, 21 feet wide and 21 feet long."* The prophetic Temple Ezekiel was shown has a square altar, a picture of God's fulfilled standard of righteousness). In the negative, it means legalism, a legalist, or a socially conventional individual. For example, if you dream of wearing square glasses it means God wants to challenge or deal with your legalistic perception.

Circle

Endless, infinite, without end and beginning, surround, siege, the vault of the heavens (Job 22:14 KJV, *"...and he walketh in the circuit of heaven."*). Dreaming of yourself wearing circle glasses means you have come to terms with a particular situation in your life.

Crisscross

It means going back and forth spiritually or mentally or inaction.

Cardinal Points

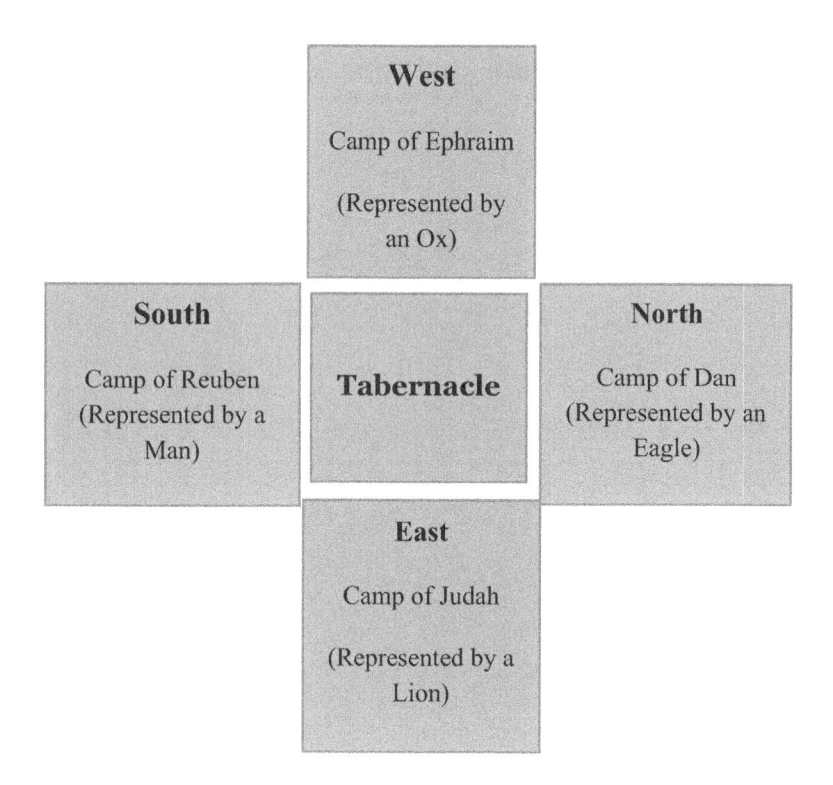

	West Camp of Ephraim (Represented by an Ox)	
South Camp of Reuben (Represented by a Man)	**Tabernacle**	**North** Camp of Dan (Represented by an Eagle)
	East Camp of Judah (Represented by a Lion)	

The camp of Israel was arranged around the Tabernacle, on the Northern side was the tribe of Dan, Naphtali, and Asher (collectively called Dan), On the Eastern side, was Judah, Issachar, and Zebulun (collectively called Judah), on the Western side was Ephraim, Manasseh and Benjamin (collectively called Ephraim) and on the Southern side was Reuben. Simeon and Gad (Collectively called Reuben). From a bird's eye view, the camp resembled a cross. In the New Testament, we have four Gospels on the account of Jesus Christ's entire ministry. The Gospel of Matthew (revealing Jesus as the Lord, Judah a Lion), the Gospel of Mark (revealing Jesus as the servant, Ephraim an Ox), the Gospel of Luke (revealing Jesus as the

Son of Man, Reuben a Man), and the Gospel of John (revealing Jesus as God, Gad the Eagle), see the diagram above.

North

That which comes from God, from above, heavenward, promotion, Christ's divine nature, biblically the Throne of God in heaven is situated in the sides of the north (Ps. 48:2), see the diagram above.

East

New beginnings, hope, a new day, anticipation of good things (the sun rises from the east). Kingship, authority, ruling, that which comes from Christ the Eastern side of Israel's camp resembled Judah which implies a Lion the king in the animal kingdom, see the diagram above.

West

The far end of the world, servant, serving, man's strength and power (the Western side of Israel's camp was the tribe of Ephraim which was represented by a picture of an Ox, see the diagram above).

South

That which comes from man, manmade, what is weak, unenduring, and temporal (the Southern side of Israel's camp was Reuben which was represented by the face of a Man).

Hearing God's voice in Dreams

Water

According to Scriptures dreaming of water means a lot of people, tongues, and nations. Rev. 17:15 GW, *"The angel also said to me, "The waters you saw, on which the prostitute is sitting, are people, crowds, nations, and languages."* It also means the gift of the Holy Spirit, life (water is the source of life), Rev. 22:17 GW, *"The Spirit and the bride say, "Come!" Let those who hear this say, "Come!" Let those who are thirsty come! Let those who want the water of life take it as a gift."*

River

It means being a source of refreshment for others (a gift that is meant to relieve and refresh i.e. a teaching ministry), spiritual satisfaction, the gift of the Holy Spirit to a believer (Joh. 7:37-38), any of the gifts of the Holy Spirit upon a believer, see 1 Cor. 12:8-10.

Well

The indwelling of the Holy Spirit in an individual, eternal life, regeneration, Joh. 4:14 KJV, *"But whosoever drinketh of the water that I shall give him shall never thirst, but the water that I shall give him shall be in him a well of water springing up into everlasting life."*).

Springwater

Rejuvenation, revival, quickening, life-giving, refreshment, and renewal (the priests in Israel always used running water, it had to be freshwater. They never used water from a dam).

Deep waters

Words from the heart, words of wisdom (Prov. 18:4a GW, *"The words of a person's mouth are like deep waters."*).

Overflowing stream

Source of wisdom (Prov. 18:4b GW, *"The fountain of wisdom is an overflowing stream."*).

Dam

A retained old anointing or revelation, a spiritual grace that has been halted, immobile, or deadlocked. The need for a fresh anointing or a fresh revelation (God commanded Israel not to store up manna but to eat fresh manna for each day a representation of a need for a fresh revelation every day. Yesterday's manna is not needed to carry you forth for today). The disciples in the book of Acts lived in a continual cycle of refilling themselves with the Holy Ghost. They did not only stop and be satisfied with the initial filling of the Holy Spirit (Acts 2:4) they continually kept themselves refilled with the Holy Spirit (Acts 4:31 & Jud. 20).

Dirty water

God exposing a demonic attack planned against you, heresy or apostasy (false teaching or doctrine).

Saltwater

Drinking or tasting saltwater means about to experience an unpleasant experience or situation, bitterness.

Boiling water

Trouble, commotion. If the water is boiling in your home it means trouble ahead for the family, if it's boiling in your house it means trouble coming against your life.

Dark water

A demonic trap or activity. It can also mean familiar spirits, the demons that masquerade themselves as your dead relatives or it might mean being followed by such spirits, see the 11th chapter of my book The Prophecy.

Seasons

Spring

God is either taking you or making you aware that you are in a season of rebirth in which plants and trees blossom and bloom, you are in a season of hope in which situations around you will turn to your favor. In the Old Testament, there were three Feasts celebrated in this season, the Passover (resurrection, dead things coming back to life in the family, business, finances, etc.), the Unleavened Bread (for seven days Israel was to eat bread without yeast, yeast representing sin, this means a season of sanctification), and the feast of the First-fruits (the sign of the nearing harvest). The Feast of Pentecost (Acts 2:1) in the Jewish called The Feast of Weeks was also around this season on the 6th of Sivan, fifty days after the Passover, this marked the harvest.

Summer

God bringing you to a season of harvesting and gathering of fruits (your sown seeds of good works, offerings, and tithes). This is normally a season of flowers (colorfulness, reproduction, and beauty).

Autumn

A season of your life where trees and plants dry. It is in this situation where you feel alone and situations seem to overwhelm you, it is here where you should be sowing seeds of confession and financial seeds—in the Jewish calendar toward the latter half beginning of the month of Tishri was the beginning of sowing. God reveals His plan for your life in this season for in the Old Testament three of Israel's Feasts were celebrated in this season. The feast of Trumpets (Rosh Hashanah 1st day of the month of Tishri, marking a season of repentance before the coming of the Day of the Lord, remembering that the Scriptural repentance is not self-chastisement or self-inflicted judgment nor condemnation. The Greek word in the New Testament means a purifying of the mind, a change of thinking, a renewing of the mind, *metanoeo*), the Day of Atonement was the second feast (Yom Teruah, on the 10th day of the month of Tishri, this signifies the Day of the Lord, it implies a season of Christ's manifestation, His grace as on this day the sins of the people would be covered in the blood of a Lamb, forgiveness, remission of sins and Christ's victory over your sins, weaknesses, and death), and on the 15th day of Tishri was the feast of Tabernacles (the feast of Booths, where all over the country Israel would camp in small booths outside the comfort of their homes. This also means God's deliverance, delivering you from your enemies and judging them. According to Bible prophecy, He will also establish His Kingdom when He is on earth in this season, thus meaning your entering in God's Kingdom, God's will for your life.

Winter

A spiritual season of indifference, lacking enthusiasm, unconcerned, lack of spiritual devotion, lack of spiritual zeal, without the passion of the spirit, and commitment, compromise, passivity toward spiritual things, dead conscience, etc. (it's a season marked with cold and in some countries, it is also followed by endless rains).

Transportation

Any mode of transportation that takes, goods or people from one place to another speaks of ministry, destiny, or business. As you will see below there are three modes of transportation. As in every aspect of dreams also in this aspect colors are important.

On land

Transport that moves on land speaks of either a local and or national ministry. Driving means being called to lead that ministry but if you are seated on the seat next to the driver this means being the assistant in that ministry, assistant to the pastor, or whoever the leader is. Assuming a seat as one of the passengers means a ministry you are currently part of or will submit to in the future.

Bicycle

A bicycle is limited to only short term distances because it uses your effort to go. So cycling a bicycle speaks of a personal ministry such as your prayer life, studying of the Word, personal intercessions, or your short journey and life in the line of purpose or a seasonal purpose (what you ought to do in that period of your life).

Motor Bike

Driving a motorcycle also speaks of a personal calling that has nothing to do with other people but needs you individually. It normally speaks of your anointing (a motorcycle needs gas to run), passion, zeal, or drive. It also means a seasonal assignment that requires spiritual acceleration.

Small car

The destiny of your family or a group of people you are either called to lead or are currently leading if you are driving it. Or it may mean a small business. If you as a small business owner dream of an SUV it means God is revealing to you the next level of growth of your business.

Van

They normally carry goods, dreaming of driving a van many times this means a small ministry you are called to lead, people, a local church, a pastoral.

Bus

Driving a bus means a big local ministry, a great number of people. This means a calling to lead a greater local ministry, a great local influence, and impact, a pastoral.

Taxi

Driving a taxi means called to lead a sizable number of people. A local ministry purposed to function within a certain local and for a particular group of people

Train

Riding a train means being part of an elongated assignment or ministry, or part of a connected sequence of people or destinies, a ministry designed to move in a sequence.

On Water

A ministry set for the nations, beyond your local borders, assigned and destined to go internationally.

Boat

Called to preach beyond your people, an international preaching ministry. It also means to plunge or dive into a certain vision or mission that overwhelms you trusting God.

Ship

A call to take the Gospel of Jesus Christ to the ends of the world, massive Evangelism.

On Air

A higher spiritual dimension, a higher spiritual vision, or a prophetic insight or calling.

Helicopter

A spiritual ministry confined within your nation. A helicopter can move in any direction, it can also move backward and hover on air. This means a higher spiritual calling that is entrusted to your total control.

Airplane

Conference speaker, an itinerant speaker, a teacher of the Word. A traveling ministry of teaching, this includes your God-given messages sent out via social media, TV, or books. Often in dreams, the aero plane is steered by the pilot and we become passengers. This means a ministry that is not within your control but depends on God's control if it happens you arrive late you might miss it, timing is of high importance in this ministry.

Private Jet

A private jet travels faster on air, it is sleek and quick. This can mean a prophetic message, a move of the Spirit on your life, or God's supernatural acceleration on a particular need in your life, it can be in health, finances, relationships, etc.

Weapons

Knife

Sharp words, insults, offending words, pejorative or derogatory speech.

Gun

A human attack instigated by demons. When pointing at you it means demonic schemes or plots targeted at you.

Ax

A sharp ax means a sharp mind, strategy, plan, or idea. It also means having an edge on something, being prepared, words of wisdom. A blunt ax means words without weight, unpreparedness, or the absence of skill.

Spear

It means to strike, being targeted, and destroy.

Arrow

Direct Satanic attacks, unbelief, doubt, fear, worry (Eph. 6:16 GW, *"In addition to all these, take the Christian faith as your shield. With it, you can put out all the flaming arrows of the evil one."*

Javelin

About to experience, be involved, or dragged into a tumult or riot.

Dagger

An attack of a dry situation specifically financially, a drought, a recession (the Hebrew word for dagger is *chereb* which is the same word used for drought).

Sword

Hearing God's voice in Dreams

The Word of God (Heb. 4:12 GW, *"God's word is living and active. It is sharper than any two-edged sword and cuts as deep as the place where soul and spirit meet, the place where joints and marrow meet. God's word judges a person's thoughts and intentions."*). See also Eph. 6:17.

Hearing God's voice in Dreams

TO THE PROPHETS OF DREAMS

In my study of the Bible, I have found by the revelation of the Holy Spirit that from the birthing to the rise and establishment of a nation God releases six anointings or we can call them Mantles. When a nation fails in rising or establishment we can always trace that to the abortion of any of the six Mantles.

The last of the six anointings is what I call the "Soom or Michah" anointing which is the Hebrew word for preservers of a nation. We will look at the Michah anointing or Preserver's Mantle from two Old Testament characters. The first being Joseph. This young man dreamt two dreams which we will look into later in this book and how they were interpreted by his brothers. By an interpretation that outlined Joseph's destiny to lead his father, mother, and his eleven brothers. Out of jealousy, his brothers sold him to slavery to try to abort God's purpose for him. Little did they know that his destiny is more important to them than it is for him when he became a ruler in Egypt, the most powerful country at the time he was the prime minister of Egypt, after a succession of a couple of tricks he finally made himself known to his brothers who did not realize him. On realizing him with faces buried in shame Joseph softly reassured them, *"Please come closer to me,"* Joseph said to his brothers. When they did so, he said, *"I am Joseph, the brother you sold into slavery in Egypt! Now, don't be sad or angry with yourselves that you sold me. God sent me ahead of you to **save lives**."* Gen. 45:4-5 GW. The King James Version states it, "to preserve life", the Hebrew word Michah.

When a nation has rejected God's standards and policies in its failure and predicaments God out of His mercy releases the Michah Mantle to preserve the nation. The second Michah Mantle we see is Daniel the prophet. As you will notice these two characters are the same in every possible way. God raises such gifts in the same pattern and they undergo the same processes and training. Daniel was one of the princes of Judah. Israel as a nation had not kept God's Sabbath years for 490 years (God required Israel to put the land to rest in every seventh year). Divide 490 by 7. The seven being for the Sabbatical year. You will get 70, meaning Israel had not kept 70 Sabbath years. Prophet Jeremiah then prophesied for over 50 years that God will bring them to captivity under Babylon until the 70 years were fulfilled. So are the writings of Daniel in captivity. God sent him with his nation to preserve it. Both Joseph and Daniel were still young boys when God sent them to captivity and both were dreamers, apart from being dreamers these young men were interpreters of dreams which consummate their calling of being the Michah's. One was Egypt, the other was Babylon. Joseph and Daniel had similar anointing and gifts but were called into two separate places.

It was in Egypt where God delivered Israel from slavery. Abraham is regarded as having fallen when he went down to Egypt. Egypt thus being the principle of the world, the enemy's territory (Pharaoh), when we say the world we mean the order of things including its people, everyone not born of God, notice, I didn't say created, *"For God so loved the world that he gave his only begotten Son..."* Joh. 3:16 KJV. To Egypt God sent Joseph, meaning his sending forth was to the unbelieving people to preserve his people the called-out ones. Some Michah Mantles will be sent out by God to the world for the benefit of the Church. Babylon being where God brought His people out of captivity, Babylon being a type of the system, the marketplace, the marketplace is anywhere where the fundamental principles of the economy are practiced. According to one of the definitions of the English dictionary *"Economy is a collective focus of the study of money, currency and trade, and the efficient use of resources."*

God sent Daniel to Babylon to preserve His people. Joseph is the Hebrew name for "God shall add another." And Daniel meaning "God the Judge." To the world (Egypt) God sends the Joseph (fruitfulness) Michah Mantle to bring forth abundance, or fruitfulness when the system fails to provide solutions and this anointing solves the crisis and problems more especially for the benefit of His people. To the system (the marketplace) God sends Daniel (God the Judge) to judge, negate, veto, and correct the structure because under normal circumstances the system is meant to oppress the weak. Anyone that is in business that individual is in spiritual warfare, money is spiritual. Every man and woman sent into entrepreneurship (company and organization startups), the sires of ideas not necessarily businessmen and women (CEOs, managers, MBAs students) it does not matter whether they are born again or not these people are sent to rise against the system. Cyrus the Great is a good example God called him to overthrow the system but he was an unbeliever, Isaiah prophesied about him 250 years before he was born:

> *This is what the LORD says about Cyrus, his anointed one: I have held him by his right hand so he could conquer the nations ahead of him, strip kings of their power, and open doors ahead of him so that the gates would not be shut. I will go ahead of you, Cyrus, and smooth out the rough places. I will break down the bronze doors and cut through the iron bars. For the sake of my servant Jacob, Israel, my chosen one, I have called you by name. I have given you a title of honor, although you don't know me. Isa. 45:1-2 & 4 GW.*

It was through Cyrus that Israel was released from the Babylonian captivity and he funded the rebuilding of God's temple in Jerusalem from his treasury.

The system can only produce consumers anyone rising to the level of a producer is immediately terrifying and overthrowing it. There are different kinds of anointing that God raises but the Michah anointing necessitates that one be born again.

Hearing God's voice in Dreams

If you have the Michah Mantle distinguish where you are sent between the world and the system. One cannot have both at once but under rare circumstances, one can have one following the other such a one can be called to the world and then later released to the system. All depends upon the individual's grace.

It is so clear that God is getting ready to send these anointing to the system and the marketplace. Some of these Mantles have been positioned across the nations of the world some are still in training. We are preparing for the greatest revival the world has ever seen. These young women and men have deep dreams and visions of the night that affect nations. And they carry a ministry that explains, decodes, and reveals mysteries and dark sayings of the spirit realm. The above are some of the few characteristics for you to check whether you are not one of them. Let us deal with more characteristics of this ministry. This is where mystery unlockers, dreamers, and prophets of dreams will meet their lingo.

The Michah Anointing Definition

הַיָחְמֶ

Hebrew reads from right to left, not like English which is from left to right. The above is the Hebrew word for Michah.

מֶ

Starting from the right the first letter is Mem, this letter represents to bind or a flow of something, being inspired.

ח

Hearing God's voice in Dreams

This second letter is Cheth, which represents marriage or a bond it is made up of a Vav left pillar which letter represents a man and Zayin right pillar which represents a woman and the Maqqeph the upper bar which represents God (Marriage, covenant or commitment to the assignment of God).

י

The third letter, this letter is a Yod a picture of an open hand representing their ability to possess leaders, influences, and peoples.

ה

The above last letter is Heh, it represents the breath or the Spirit of God. This was the letter God added to Abram's name so that it was Abraham and Sarai's name so it was changed to Sarah revealing God breathing over their lives

In simple terms, this anointing binds (Mem), connects people to God (Cheth), is possessive economically (Yod, an open hand), and conquers influences (Heh) over nations and currencies. The Mem is an open Mem, not a closed Mem. The open Mem is said to reveal the open truth of God as revealed by Moses and the closed Mem is said to reveal closed truth as seen through the Messiah the revealer of mysteries. This being their ability to interpret dreams, seasons, and decipher hidden messages of God.

Calling of the Michah

This anointing is called by God though it can be taught by men especially the area of dream interpretation can be a skill (craft), Dan. 1:17 Darby, *"God gave them knowledge and skill in all learning and wisdom, and Daniel had understanding in all visions and dreams."*). It can also be imparted through association, remember Daniel's friends, Abednego, Shadrack, and Meshack.

Assignment of the Michah Anointing

They are called to preserve nations under slavery or any oppressive system many times when the nation has rebelled against a Prophet.

Preparation

God prepares these individuals at an early age via the marketplace, For Joseph, it was in prison and for Daniel, it was through the king's government internship program.

Character

- Favorable
- Wise
- Intelligent

Structure

- Prophetic
- Administrative
- Wisdom (Marketplace connoisseur)

Their Mantle

Mystery revealers (Studying and the ability to interpret the times and dreams). They can interpret people's dreams, visions, and the writings on the wall.

Lag Time

Their ministry begins at the end of the Prophetic season when the nation did not heed the message of the Prophet. In the case of Daniel, it was after Jeremiah.

As a South African, I feel entitled to say South Africa has only tasted the first of the six Mantles. We still have a long way to go. As an African, I believe in these last days God is going to revive our beautiful continent to the full potential it was divinely intended for. I believe this Michah anointing will shift and project our African economy to highs we only saw possible in our dreams. Africa has always played a significant part in the Bible.

Let's consider this excerpt from the second chapter of the book of Genesis, *"The Lord planted a garden eastward of Eden."* Now a river went out of Eden to water the garden, and from there it parted and became four river heads. The name of the first was Pishon (anciently in the land of Babylon, modern-day Iraq), this is the one which skirts the whole land of Havilah, where there is gold, onyx, and bdellium. The gold of that land is good. And the second river is Gihon, this is the river which went around the whole land of Cush (Ethiopia). Ethiopia is in Africa, Gihon thus supplied the African continent.

This gives us more information to conclude that Africa was watered by a river from Eden which word means "The Presence of God". It is safe to assume that Africa was one of the continents surrounding the Garden of Eden. In Genesis, we continue being shown that God created animals in that garden for the first man to name them. No place has more wild animals than the African continent. This is proof that Africa has a special place in God's purpose and creation, which purpose Satan has thwarted as a result there have not been people since the world began more oppressed than the Jews and blacks.

Scholars and geologists have tried locating the Garden of Eden with no promising results. This has been due to what geologists refer to as a shift in tectonic plates and shreds of evidence left imprinted in the sedimentary rock supposedly because of a flood that some happen to believe happened thousands of years back that some scholars attribute to the flood of Noah. Africans, embrace yourselves for the coming change.

Bonus Chapter

This bonus chapter is due to the promise I made in the 10th chapter.

This is for those who can't speak in other tongues. This can be achieved in two ways, one can either be to go to a pastor or any church leader that operates in this gift through being ministered to and the laying on of hands one will receive the gift, Act 8:17-18 GW, *"Then Peter and John placed their hands on them, and the Samaritans received the Holy Spirit. Simon saw that the Spirit was given to the Samaritans when the apostles placed their hands on them."* And Act 19:6 Darby, *"And Paul having laid his hands on them, the Holy Spirit came upon them, and they spoke with tongues and prophesied."*

The gift of speaking in tongues is attributed to receiving the Holy Spirit. A believer is to receive the Holy Spirit twice, the first instance is when you accepted Jesus Christ as your Lord and Savior He indwells you (He permanently lives in you), this we call regeneration (born again, see Joh. 3:3-8), it is when the Holy Spirit comes in you and recreates your spirit which was dead because of Adam's fall, 2 Cor. 5:17 Darby, *"So if anyone be in Christ, there is a new creation; the old things have passed away; behold all things have become new."* Here, He comes bearing the nature of Christ, the fruits of the spirit (Gal. 5:22-23, Rom. 5:5).

When laid hands to receive the Holy Spirit for tongues the Bible calls this the empowerment to do the works of ministry or call it being empowered for service, teaching, prophesying, healing the sick, etc., simply put operating in the Gifts of the Holy Spirit. Acts 1:8 Weymouth, *"and yet you will receive **power** when the Holy Spirit has come **upon** you, and you will be my witnesses in Jerusalem and all Judaea and Samaria and to the remotest parts of the earth."* The Greek word for power here is *dunamis* meaning a miracle-working power.

Tongues are also for you to minister power, signs and wonders, and miracles to others. You do not have to tarry as the 120 disciples tarried in Jerusalem to receive the gift. Since then the Holy Spirit has never left the earth. Just lock the door of your room and lift your hands and ask God for this precious gift, say, *"Father, I thank you that you always hear me, I pray you to give me the Holy Spirit upon for the work of the ministry, you said in Luke 11:13, 'If therefore *ye*, being evil, know how to give good gifts to your children, how much rather shall the Father who is of heaven give the Holy Spirit to them that ask him?' I receive the gift of the Holy Spirit right now in Jesus' Name."*

Begin to thank God and receive it by faith, notice what Acts 2 verse 4 says, *"And they were all filled with the Holy Ghost, and **began to speak with other tongues**, as the Spirit gave them utterance."* Darby. Because you have asked God for the Holy Spirit He has given you so begin to speak in other tongues. The verse above says the disciples began to speak with other tongues. It was the disciples who began not the Holy Spirit. As you begin according to the above verse He will give you utterance (inspiration). What you feel does not matter, we walk not by senses but by faith (2 Cor. 5:7), though others had felt like butterflies in their bellies, some like rivers of water welling up inside them (Joh. 7:37-38). If you feel nothing it doesn't mean a thing.

Begin to enjoy your victorious Christian journey.

Please do give us a book review on Amazon. Your review is important to us. Thank you.

Reference List

Nicholas V. Mbanjwa, *Discover the Force behind Creativity*, The Meaning and the Purpose of Life, ISBN 978 – 0 – 620 – 69970 – 9, 2016, South Africa

Nicholas V. Mbanjwa, *The Prophecy*, The Meaning and the Purpose of Life, ISBN 978-1-674-31983-4, 2019, South Africa.

Kenneth E. Hagin, *I Believe in Visions*, ISBN 978-0892765089, Faith Library Publications, U.S.A

Chuck Missler, *Revelation Notes*, ISBN 1- 880532- 03 -9, Koinonia House Inc, 2006, U.S.A

Watchman Nee, *Aids to "Revelation"*. ISBN 0-935008-60-8, Christian Fellowship Publishers, Inc, 1983, U.S.A

Chuck Missler, *Exodus Notes,* and ISBN 1 – 57821 – 083 – 6, Koinonia House Inc, 1999, U.S.A

The Rev John McClintock D.D., and James Strong S.T.D., *Cyclopedia of Biblical, Theological and Ecclesiastical Literature*, 1895.

Strong's Hebrew and Greek Dictionaries, Dictionaries of Greek and Hebrew words taken from Strong's Exhaustive Concordance by James Strong, S.T.D., LL.D. 1890.

The English Dictionary 1.2.2, Wiktionary texts under CC-BY-SA license according to the Wikimedia Foundation licensing policy.

The Cambridge Bible for Schools and Colleges, Cambridge University Press, 1882-1992

Don Fleming, *Bridgeway Bible Commentary*, ISBN 0 947342 72 9, 1988, 1994, 2005 https://www.space.com/20320-astronaut-jim-lovell-apollo-13-biography.html

J.S.M Matsebula (History of Swaziland) p.13.

Another Book by the Author

Back in 2015 God pressed it heavily in my spirit to write a book on the two fundamental doctrines of Christianity, Soteriology (Doctrine of Salvation) and Eschatology (The Doctrine of Bible Prophecy).

I sensed an extreme urgency for the book for what was ahead.

In 2019 I sensed the same thing and finally wrote the book, The Prophecy. It didn't sell at all when I advertised it. But on Amazon U.S it had just a few sales. I questioned myself if did I really hear from God.

When the Covid 19 hit, people where so fearful and uncertain the book seemed to pick up on Amazon sales. The issue of the Covid exposed the Church on the ignorance of Bible Prophecy. People thought it was a sign of Christ's Second coming and the vaccine the mark of the beast.

This book answers everything about the end times and the Covid-19 isn't one of them and Bill Gates not the Antichrist. It explains who he is, where he will come from and when.

I care not whether you think Bible Prophecy isn't important but this outbreak exposed us to our ignorance of it, arm yourself with knowledge, knowledge is freedom. You can order a copy or an eBook on Amazon.

Made in the USA
Las Vegas, NV
19 September 2023